KATHLEEN PETYARRE

Wakefield Press
17 Rundle Street, Kent Town, South Australia 5067

First published 2001

Gallery photographs by Clayton Glen Photography
Designed by Liz Nicholson, design BITE
Printed and bound by Hyde Park Press

Kathleen Petyarre is represented by Gallerie Australis, Adelaide.

National Library of Australia
Cataloguing-in-publication entry

Nicholls, Christine (Christine Judith).
Kathleen Petyarre: genius of place.
Bibliography.
ISBN 1 86254 547 2.
ISBN 1 86254 546 4 (pbk).
1. Petyarre, Kathleen. 2. Art, Australian aboriginal. 3.Aborigines, Australian - Art - 20th century. I. North, Ian, 1945- . II. Title

709.94074

The expression 'genius of place' is from the poet Virgil:
'Geniumque loci . . . precatur', 'Implored the genius of place'.

This series of books showcasing the works of South Australian living artists is initiated by the SALA Week committe and is published with the assistance of the Government of South Australia through Arts South Australia. This is the second book in the series, following *Annette Bezor: A Passionate Gaze*, 2000.

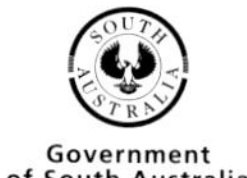

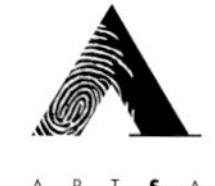

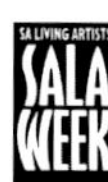

Wakefield Press thanks Arts South Australia for its continued support.

Important Note - In Australian Aboriginal communities the usual practice is neither to name nor reproduce visual images of the recently deceased. Where such references and images have been reproduced in this book, appropriate Indigenous protocols and permissions have been followed. Discretion and care should nevertheless be exercised when displaying the book in Central Australia. Finally, to the authors' knowledge, no restricted or secret/sacred images or information have been included in this book.

Front cover: *Mountain Devil Lizard Dreaming (Sandstorm) 2000* (page 73)
Back cover: *Mountain Devil Lizard Dreaming - Sandhill Country (After Hailstorm) 1999* (page 71)

KATHLEEN PETYARRE

Genius of Place

Essays by Christine Nicholls
and Ian North

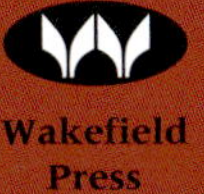

Wakefield
Press

CONTENTS

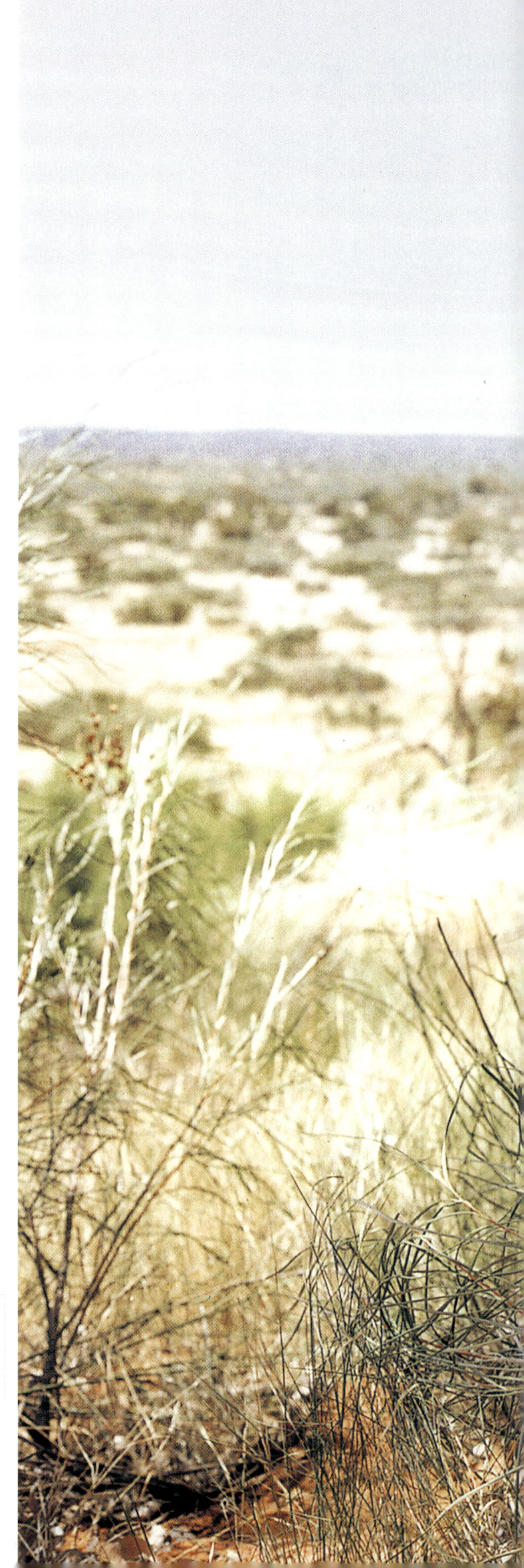

Kathleen Petyarre looking across Atnangker country, Northern Territory, December 2000

Photograph by Ian North

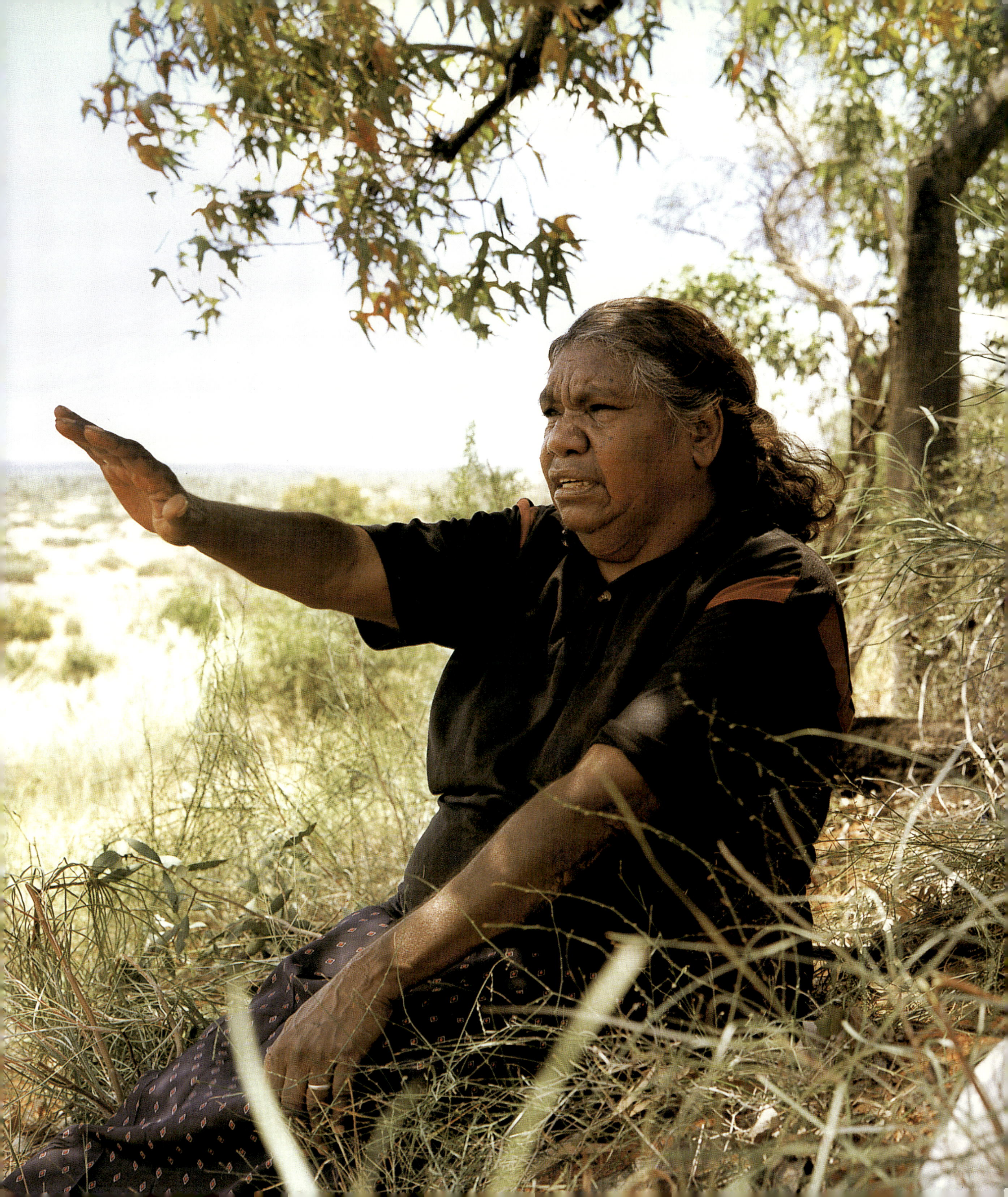

The Life and Art of Kathleen Petyarre

Author's Note

To appreciate the trajectory of Kathleen Petyarre's artistic career it is illuminating to learn something of the key events of her remarkable life. The inseparability of Kathleen's art from her life becomes evident in the telling of her story. Or, perhaps it is more accurate to speak of the several lives that Kathleen Petyarre has compressed into the space of a single lifespan. My synoptic account of Kathleen's life is based on conversations with her over a period of six years.

In the following essay I have sometimes referred to the artist by what she describes as her 'bush name', or personal name, 'Kweyetwemp', and on other occasions as 'Kathleen', or 'Petyarre', and sometimes as 'Kathleen Petyarre'. The reason for this lack of standardisation is that 'Petyarre' is not a surname but a skin name, and the name 'Kathleen' has been imposed upon her. Aboriginal personal names are not normally used either as a form of address or on a daily basis. I have taken this stance out of respect for Anmatyerr naming practices, and because I do not wish to contribute further to their assimilation to Anglo-European naming practices.

While I may not have always succeeded in doing so, throughout my essay I have tried to remain faithful to presenting Kathleen Petyarre's own perspectives on her art, life and artistic career, rather than imposing my readings on it.

This essay is based on interviews with Kathleen Petyarre, and unless otherwise cited, the direct quotes in the text are statements made to me by Kathleen in the course of our continuing conversations about her art and life.

Kweyetwemp Petyarre

When I was a little girl my grandmother mob, all the old women, showed me and taught me the ceremonies – the whole lot – they taught me singing, dancing, body painting . . . the old ladies got me to dance from when I was little one – they thought one day I would be leader.

Located approximately 270 kilometres north-east of Alice Springs in the Northern Territory, Atnangker is arid spinifex country, hilly in places and covered with low-lying vegetation, extending over more than 200 square kilometres. Hot and dry in summer, with temperatures soaring well into the fifties, Atnangker's sandy red earth is able to sustain life on account of a number of permanent water and rock holes, as well as other semi-permanent water supplies, including creek beds and underground water. During the wet season, Atnangker country is sometimes transformed by flooding rains and ferocious hailstorms. When the large hailstones are scattered over Atnangker country, the ground temporarily transforms in colour from its usual vivid red to a murky, whitish shade.

Atnangker is where Eastern Anmatyerr artist Kathleen Petyarre was born around 1940. 'Kweyetwemp' was the name bestowed on the baby girl of the Petyarre skin group. Almost a decade later the child Kweyetwemp was re-named 'Kathleen' following her first encounter with whites. At that time Petyarre's entire extended family were arbitrarily assigned the Anglo-European names by which they are known today outside of their Anmatyerr family. Today Kathleen describes 'Kweyetwemp' as her 'bush name'.

As a small child Kweyetwemp Petyarre walked around her father's homelands with her extended family: her grandparents, her father and his three wives, her four brothers and six sisters, and also, from time to time, the children's uncles and other assorted relatives. Kweyetwemp's father was the father of all the siblings. In about 1942 Kweyetwemp's mother, Ntyerlampek Pwerle, gave birth to a second daughter, Gloria Petyarre, a full sister to Kathleen. Today Gloria Petyarre is also highly regarded as an artist and has exhibited widely.

Kweyetwemp's family group moved around their vast estate according to the systematic principles of rotational land navigation, based on the seasonal availability of water and local bush foods: emus, kangaroos, echidnas, perenties (small lizards), blue tongue lizards, goannas, witchetty and other small grubs, sugarbag and other bush honeys, bush beans, native peas, yams and acacia coriacea or dogwood seeds, which were dried and added to water to make a rather sweet milky drink. The women in the family also collected the seeds of mulga bushes and pigweed, which they would grind and then sometimes cook to make small cake-like dampers. This was a very labour intensive activity with a relatively small yield, but according to Kathleen the small seedcakes were 'delicious', and the children always looked forward to eating them.

Jeannie Devitt (1988:130–147) explains that there were at least seven, and sometimes even eight, separate stages of traditional Anmatyerr/Alyawarr seed processing: collecting the seeds, then threshing, winnowing, yandying – separating the seed from other matter like sand or other impurities – parching (for tree seeds), pounding, grinding and then, finally, cooking, which was optional. Devitt alludes to the skill needed in certain parts of the process, noting, for example, that the 'complex yandying techniques were only performed by women over the age of 50 years' and explaining that the laboratory where she sent 'unprocessed seeds for analysis had great difficulty separating crushed seed from residue . . . and were most interested in how it had been achieved traditionally' (*Ibid*:135). The latter comment points to the extreme complexity of the process, and may explain in part the willingness of Anmatyerr women, many years down the track, to learn the similarly complex and multi-faceted processes involved in batik making.

The Petyarre children developed a finely tuned, seasonally adjusted knowledge of the location of the specific plants, animals and rockholes and other water sources on their family's estate. They also acquired knowledge about the spatial history of their country, including sites of spiritual and cultural significance. To this day, Kathleen's facility in land-navigation is reflected in her artistic production. This apparently astonishing ability to reconstruct, from memory, detailed and accurate mental maps of her childhood terrain has remained with Kathleen throughout her life.

Such ability – to orientate oneself in space by envisioning a large tract of land as an entity that comprises smaller parcels of land, then conjuring up the whole in abstract form and reproducing it visually – was necessary for survival. In fact, successful land navigation and its corollary, the capacity for accurate location of food and water were essential for group survival. Collectively these invocations of large stretches of 'country' constitute 'aerial views' of particular tracts of land. The specialised and proprietal knowledge on which this skill is founded constitutes the legal–judicial foundation of Anmatyerr land-based epistemology. Anmatyerr and other Central Australian Indigenous representational practices are spatially specific reconstructions of this knowledge. Kweyetwemp Petyarre acquired this skill to a high level of competency during those early years spent in the bush and she maintains it now by painting her country on a regular basis.

It was also during this early, formative period of her life in the 1940s that Petyarre embarked upon a

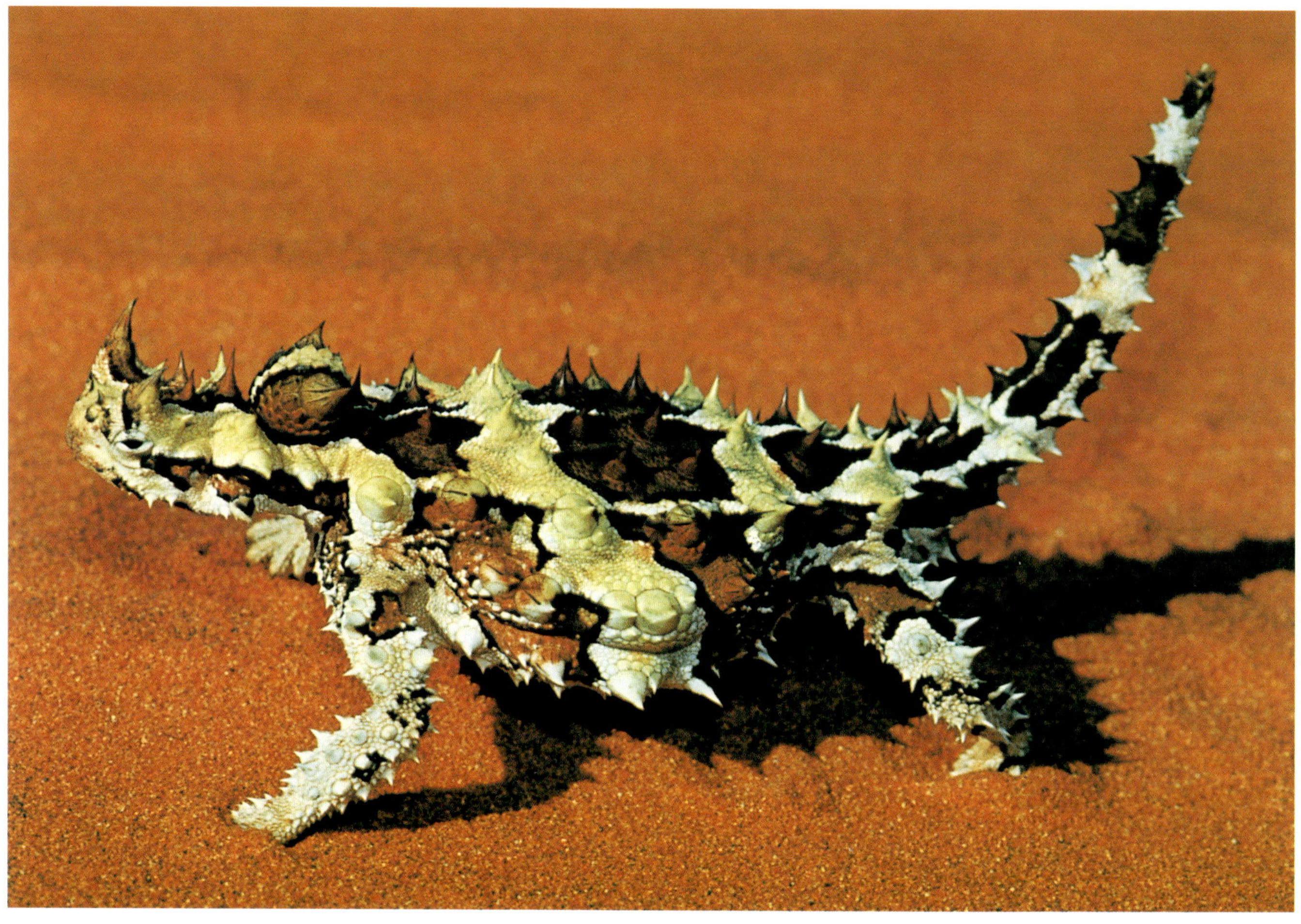

Arnkerrth, the Mountain or Thorny Devil *(Moloch horridus)* Photograph courtesy Hans Boessem, Todd Camera Store, Alice Springs, Northern Territory

classical Anmatyerr education, in which her paternal grandmother played a prominent role. Kathleen's grandmother began instructing her in what is today recognised as Petyarre's great artistic subject: almost all of her canvasses are artistic expressions of the journeying of her Dreaming Ancestor, *Arnkerrth*, the Old Woman Mountain Devil, throughout the physical and spiritual geography of her birthplace, Atnangker.

Arnkerrth, The Mountain Devil

Arnkerrth, the thorny or mountain devil, the Latin name for which is *Moloch horridus*, is a small agamid lizard with spikes on its back that inhabits the spinifex sand plains and sand ridges of the deserts and semi-deserts of Australia's interior. The mountain devil's spikes give it a striking appearance rather like a bonsai dinosaur. Were it not a diminutive creature of only eight to fourteen centimetres in length, it could star in a B-grade horror movie. *Arnkerrth*'s diet consists almost entirely of obligate ants, mainly very small *Iridomyrmex* ants.

Shy and timid, *Arnkerrth* moves slowly with a jerky motion that leaves a characteristic pattern of semi-circular tracks. This pattern of movement is – subliminally at least – evident in Kathleen's artistic works. Mountain devils are able to freeze *in situ* while walking, even with a foot off the ground. They will do this if they spot a potential predator. They can

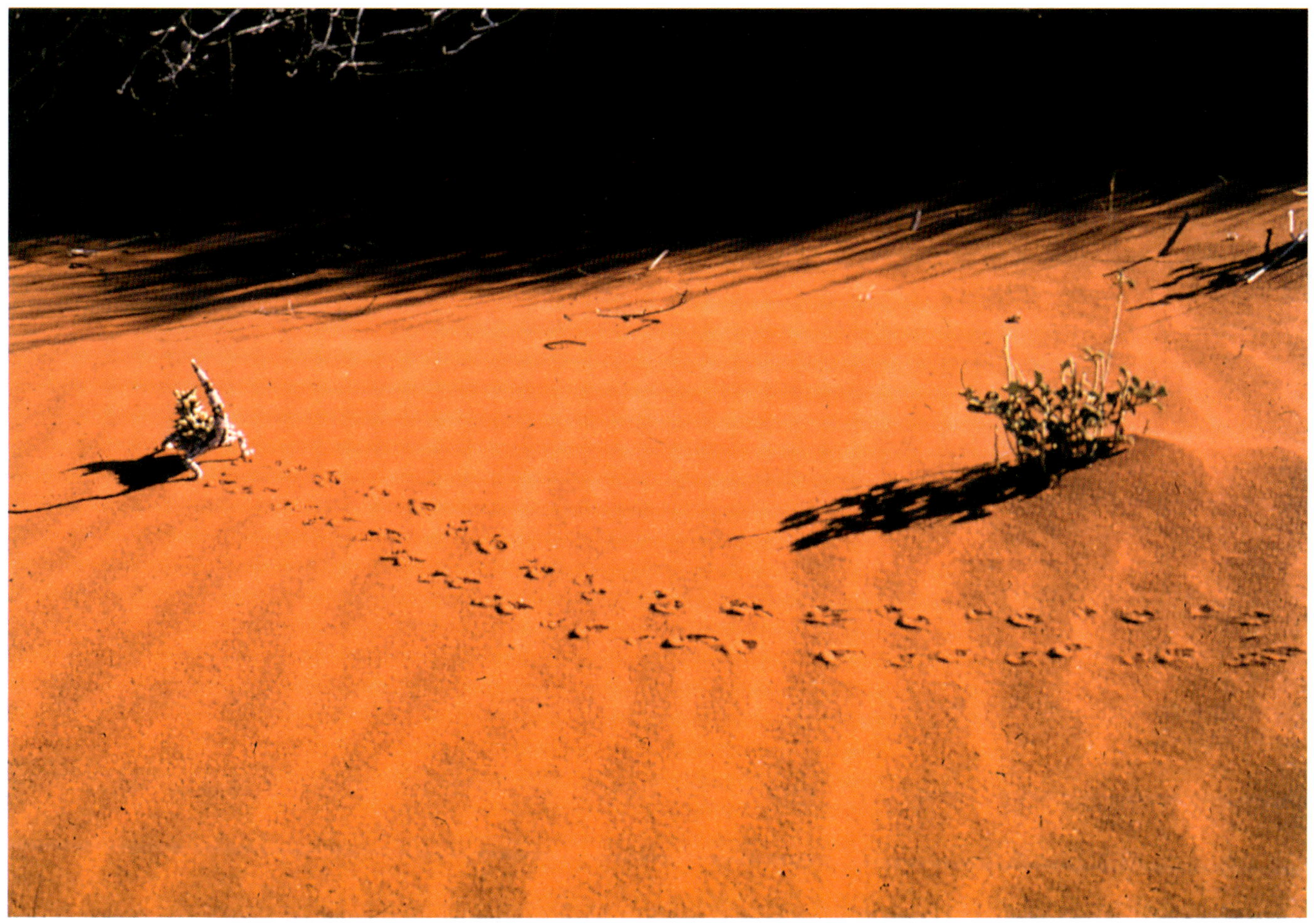

Moloch horridus, the Mountain or Thorny Devil, tracks in the sand Photograph courtesy Eric R. Pianka, School of Biological Sciences, University of Texas, Austin, Texas, United States of America

also change colour very rapidly from a normal pale ochre-like yellow and red through a succession of brighter versions of the same hues when they are warm, active and unthreatened. If it is cold or they feel threatened they are able to change through the colour range to dull, drab olive shades. By taking on the tones of the surrounding land and bushes, *Arnkerrth* enhances its chances of survival in the harsh desert conditions.

Arnkerrth also has the unusual ability to take water without drinking conventionally. Mountain devils have a hygroscopic system of grooves in their skin that leads to the corners of their mouths, and they use a gulping oral mechanism to move water along the grooves and into their mouths. They can actually drink water from the dew that falls on their backs, allowing them to withstand droughts and the other very dry climatic conditions that typify Australia's arid interior. They are able to absorb as much as a gram of water during a rainstorm.

During the early stage of her life in the bush, under the guidance of the senior women in her family, Kathleen Petyarre developed her expertise as a highly skilled practical ethologist and started accumulating her formidable knowledge of the behaviour patterns of *Arnkerrth*, her Dreaming Ancestor. *Arnkerrth*'s astonishing powers of self-camouflage, its bizarre but highly effective means of ingesting water, its incidence in the sandhills and sandy loam desert soils of the Anmatyerr and Alyawarr homelands, its idiosyncratic ambulatory style and its deserved reputation as a formidable survivor are palpable themes in Kathleen Petyarre's canvases today.

In Kathleen's art, as is the case with other Anmatyerr, Centralian, and Western Desert artistic production, *Arnkerrth* is not represented figuratively, but conceptualised spatially. In Anmatyerr art all living creatures, including human beings, are depicted as predominantly spatial rather than psychological beings, interacting in natural and cultural landscapes that occupy space over time. Kathleen's paintings of *Arnkerrth*'s journeys during the Creation era known in English as 'The Dreaming' are founded on specialised cartographic techniques that enable insiders to derive a great deal from the available visual-spatial information. The spatial information or patterns that Kathleen creates in her art correspond to and can be mapped onto existing geographic features in Atnangker country, for example the rockholes, hills and mulga spreads that *Arnkerrth* encountered in the course of her epic travels during the Dreaming. Satellite imagery and computer-generated overlays indicate a surprisingly close correspondence to the work of traditionally oriented Indigenous artists, including that of Kathleen Petyarre.

But Kathleen's paintings, like those of her countrymen and women, are more than simple reconstructions of visible spatial features. These paintings offer an *integrated* spatial, environmental, economic, spiritual and moral 'reading' of the land, of Anmatyerr spatial history, if you like. Abstract spatial features such as socio-political units and boundaries, temporal events that can be linked to spatial features, organisational events, for instance initiation ceremonies, and a high level of environmental know-how are also incorporated into the paintings, in a condensed fashion. Each work is accompanied by an elaborate and lengthy oral narrative, the retelling of which can take hours, and which custodians may sing, dance and paint. The paintings are visual, iconic metaphors for these longer narratives, which may be re-created via a variety of different art forms.

Kathleen's *Arnkerrth* (Old Woman Mountain Devil) Dreaming Narrative

The Dreaming narrative over which Kathleen and her sisters and brothers have custodial rights – although Kathleen's brothers own a different section of this highly gendered narrative – details the significant landforms and the seasonal availability of food and water on Atnangker. The narrative is an elaboration on the best methods of journeying the length and breadth of that country without compromising survival. It is also a moral treatise that explores the question of what constitutes appropriate relationships between older and younger members of Anmatyerr society, condemning rampant individualism, selfishness and impatience as characteristics antipathetic to survival in the desert. It also posits the need for induction ceremonies for young women (and by extension, for young men) to keep them from acting purely in self-interest and thereby posing a threat to group survival. Within the framework of this narrative, it is clear that Kathleen's identification with the Old Woman *Arnkerrth*, her Dreaming Ancestor, is absolute. Dreaming Ancestors may be tracts of land, watercourses, animals, vegetables or humans, and they have the capacity to change from one form, shape or state into another, and then back again. Kathleen and her Dreaming Ancestor *Arnkerrth* are one and the same being.

Kathleen Petyarre explains a section of her Dreaming narrative in this way:

That Arnkerrth is one Old Lady, my Dreaming Ancestor, who was travelling all the time to a big mountain . . . called in English Mt Bullocky, called in my language Apmakweng, big apwert [hill]. That old Arnkerrth girl she bin dancing there, she was dancing for herself, a ceremony just for herself, one lady alone, one lady dancing all alone. When that day she came back from Apmakweng, to big mountain Alhalker, in the afternoon [she was] a little bit late, and she saw everybody else had gone, other mob had disappeared. That Arnkerrth woman saw that all the family, brothers and sisters, man mob, woman mob, had gone away, had gone travelling, they hadn't waited for her. She said, 'Aahhh, that mob all gone!' . . . She was a sulky one! Really sulky one! That old Arnkerrth woman said, 'Oh – you fellas bin leave me!' and she sat down and sulked and then she thought up a plan: she decided to catch all the young girls. She wanted to catch them and show them who was the boss!

Kathleen explains that the reason the Old Woman Mountain Devil became so irritated when she found that her countrymen and women had not waited for her as promised was the threat that such careless abandonment posed to *group* survival. The person with the greatest knowledge of the terrain – in this case, the Old Woman *Arnkerrth* – was the one for whom it was essential that the others waited, because ultimately the survival of all was dependent on her detailed knowledge of the physical and cultural terrain. *Arnkerrth* was not simply seeking revenge or acting punitively in wanting to catch the young girls and teach them a lesson they would be unlikely to forget. Survival in the desert is predicated on the reliability of *all* members of the group, and as young people seem unable, or unwilling, to absorb this simple lesson by osmosis, they need to be *taught* it in a structured, formal context. This is why there is a continuing need for ceremonies for both young men and women, during which dependability is drummed into them, inculcated into their habitual thinking to the point where it becomes automatic, second nature, part of the social contract.

As Kathleen concludes: 'This Old Lady Arnkerrth Dreaming – my Dreaming – shows us about the business for all the young Anmatyerr girls. Our Law.'

Kathleen began acquiring her knowledge of *Arnkerrth* Dreaming when as a small child she listened to her paternal grandmother's verbal account of the narrative, and also to the related narratives of the Green Bean, Bush Seeds and *Atwakey* (Wild Orange or *Capparis Mitchelli*, which Kathleen describes as 'little orange bush tucker'). The child also observed how her grandmother visually represented *Arnkerrth*, watching her paint the *awely* designs associated with that Dreaming on the bodies of other women, using a black paint made from dried bush plums and yellow, red and white ochres. Gradually, over time, Kathleen earned the right to depict, interpret and teach others about the *Arnkerrth* Dreaming narrative through a variety of different media. It is to the latter phase that the young Kweyetwemp aspired as a young child, and now, as an adult, is recognised as having reached.

Petyarre's sensitivity to and knowledge about her Dreaming Ancestor is the result of a long formal education in the Law and culture of the Anmatyerr. But like all children, the Petyarre brothers and sisters also played and interacted with one another in ways that reflected their developing personalities. Kweyetwemp was, by her own account, a spirited, feisty little girl:

When I was . . . little, most of the time I was quiet . . . but I remember [that] sometimes I was a cheeky little girl. I used to hit my little sisters Violet and Nancy! One time I dragged my little sister Gloria by the hair when I'd found a goanna out in the bush – she took my goanna away from me – so I grabbed Gloria by her hair and I pulled it hard! My mother stopped us. She said, 'You two fellas stop fighting! You have to eat that goanna separate!' So we ate the goanna separate.

Like other Indigenous Australian people, during times of abundant food the family would link up with other family groups for important ceremonies, including increase rituals and men's initiation ceremonies and women's *awely* ceremonies. Kathleen Petyarre spoke to the linguist Jenny Green about the process of being painted up for those ceremonies:

Awely ingkwernetyart arelh ampwel-rnem werlaty-angkwarr arrernemel, iltyel arrernemel, arrernemel iltyelek-amparr werlaty arrpenh-angkwarr, and inweng-angkwarr arrernemel iltyel, an tyepalel arrernemel. Iyleperek atherr arrernem, white one atherr iltya atherr arrernem, iltyel ingkwernem iyleperek, kel tyepalel anem ingkwernemel. Urlpa then arrernem ngwenty-ngwenty then, alakenh arrernemel, kel iyleper aketh imernt urntemel. Kel arelh ampwa pwath urntemel, kweter-akert, arrkarlp-akert, urntemel kweter ingkernemel ra . . . Arelh ingwer-rnem akenh aylelhanerleng . . . Aperl-aperl atha aretyart, aperl-aperlel akalty-anthetyart urntep-urnterleng. Well ayeng aperl atyenh-apeny anem akalty-irrek.

The old women used to paint the ceremonial designs on the breasts, first with their fingers, on the breasts and chest, and then with a brush called a tyepal, made from a twig. They paint the thighs with white paint, with their fingers and then with the tyepal. They paint up with red and white ochres, then they dance, showing their thighs. While the other women are singing the old 'boss' woman dances with a ceremonial stick and a headdress of feathers, and she places the ceremonial stick in the earth . . . I used to watch my father's mother, and she used to instruct me as I was dancing. Well now I have learnt about it, like my father's mother.[1]

The centrally located, adjacent men and women's ceremonial grounds where these ceremonies take place are depicted in a number of Kathleen's paintings, as if configured from a bird's-eye perspective (see diagram page 15). Because of the distance from which the ceremonial ground is observed, and owing to the human eye's limited power of resolution, there is a concomitant loss of detail. The panoramic viewpoint taken by Petyarre in her works results in the men and women's business areas visually approximating a bisected quadrilateral.

The ceremonies continue to be held on those sites, on a yearly basis, usually around Christmas. In the old days the ceremonies were always timed to coincide with the ripening and proliferation of that staple bush vegetable, the yam, or sweet potato. For Petyarre the yam is redolent of the halcyon days when she and her family lived in the bush free from white dominion. As a means of evoking the irretrievable past, the eidetic yam is as powerfully mnemonic to Kathleen Petyarre as the legendary madeleine was to Proust:

We would have ceremony when there were yams, ripe yams; we would have big ceremony every year when the yams were ripe. Eating yams! Every year when the yams were ripe – we would dance, sing, paint up.

Also, when I was a little girl my grandmother mob, all the old women, showed me and taught me the ceremonies – the whole lot – taught me singing, dancing, body painting . . . old ladies got me to dance from when I was little one – they thought one day I would be leader. Our grandmother and our other grandmother taught us awely, me and Violet, when we were about this big [using her hands to indicate a child of about seven or eight years old]. Our family had a really big ceremony then, before the whitefella.

Meeting a White Man

As Kathleen tells it, not long after one particularly memorable ceremony involving her entire extended family, a happy occasion when everyone feasted on tender young yams, Kweyetwemp and her family came across a white person for the first time. This was in the late 1940s. For a while the family had heard rumours about the presence of whites in their area, and Kathleen remembers the extended family hiding behind bushes watching white people walking past. Despite the fact that pastoralists were reasonably well-established in adjacent country by the late 1940s, Kathleen does not recall meeting any 'whitefellas' face to face before this time.

She says that by Anmatyerr standards the first white man she remembers meeting seemed strange. At that time she had no way of knowing that the fellow probably was quite peculiar, judged even by the (at that stage) unfathomable criteria of the white interlopers. In many respects, both the man himself and that early encounter seem to have become mythologised in Kathleen's mind in a way that typifies adult recollections of early childhood experiences, in which one often has difficulty unravelling fact from fiction, and where contradictions become apparent.

This hazy figure from Kathleen's childhood was wandering around Petyarre's family's land accompanied only by a camel of unknown origin. Kathleen has a number of theories about the man's identity. She thinks that perhaps he was a former army officer stationed near her family's country during the second world war. Solitary and reclusive, perhaps the man had chosen not to return home after the war was over, but instead to remain on Anmatyerr land.

The man sponged off Petyarre's family, who generously provided him with bush tucker over an extended period of time. They felt an obligation to look after him because, at that time, in Kathleen's words, 'there was no flour, no flour and no sugar', and they didn't want to feel responsible for the man starving to death or dying of thirst.

But despite the man's dependence on the kindness of strangers for his own continuing survival, he strongly objected to the family's nudity. Kathleen recalls that his moral stance on their nakedness led to his insistence that even the youngest family members wear clothes regardless of the weather. The family complied with the man's adjuration to don clothing. This symbolised the change in power relations that had come with the white interlopers. The family sensed that the new world into which they had been catapulted by the forces of history was there to stay.

Today, Kathleen Petyarre remembers with amusement her entire extended family being outfitted in itchy, ill-fitting army supply clothes. The man importuned them to wear this inappropriate garb even in the scorchingly hot Anmatyerr summers, when temperatures regularly soared to more than 50°C in the shade:

First we girls had to wear little army shorts, little boys' army shorts, and then later times we girls had to wear sacks, flour bags and other bags with cut out hole for neck and arms – we had to wear them [laughing]. Really itchy one.

Kathleen talks of this period of her life without rancour, despite her clear recollections of the unpleasant prickling of rough fabric against her skin in the intense summer heat. She finds the man, his attitudes and his antics highly entertaining. Equally, Kathleen is dismissive of any criticism – including mine – of the petty tyranny exerted by this mean-spirited loner over her family. She glosses over the disruption that the man caused when he turned up as an uninvited guest on their land and started laying down a new and different law.

Indeed, the youthful Kweyetwemp found her inaugural meeting with a white person deeply fascinating. She says that she still often thinks about it today, more than half a century later. That first crossing of paths sparked in Kathleen an enduring curiosity about social mores and lifeways other than her own. Her lifelong interest in the habits and cultural practices of non-Indigenous people began at the moment of that first beguiling concurrence. Over the years Kathleen's interest in non-Indigenous people has developed into an engrossment that has never waned. It has prompted in her a desire to work and otherwise interact closely with non-Indigenous people in a variety of settings. While Kathleen brings acute, almost forensically sharp powers of observation to her interactions with white people, she remains, for the most part, non-judgemental.

Gradually, after that initial encounter with 'the Colonising Other', Petyarre's family and others like them were partly coerced, partly seduced, into a more sedentary way of life following relocation within their own country, initially to the pastoral properties that had become well-established by that time. Undoubtedly with heavy-handed irony, the white newcomers had re-named the area 'Utopia'. (See Richardson 2001 for more on this.)

During Kathleen Petyarre's teenage years, the family worked for the pastoralists in the region, doing stock work, cooking and odd jobs, for which they were 'paid' in rations. This mirrored the experience of many other Indigenous families in northern Australia. Later they, like other Anmatyerr families in the region, were pressured into taking up residence in the newly created government settlements that were springing up on their country, underpinned by the policy of assimilation for Aboriginal people.

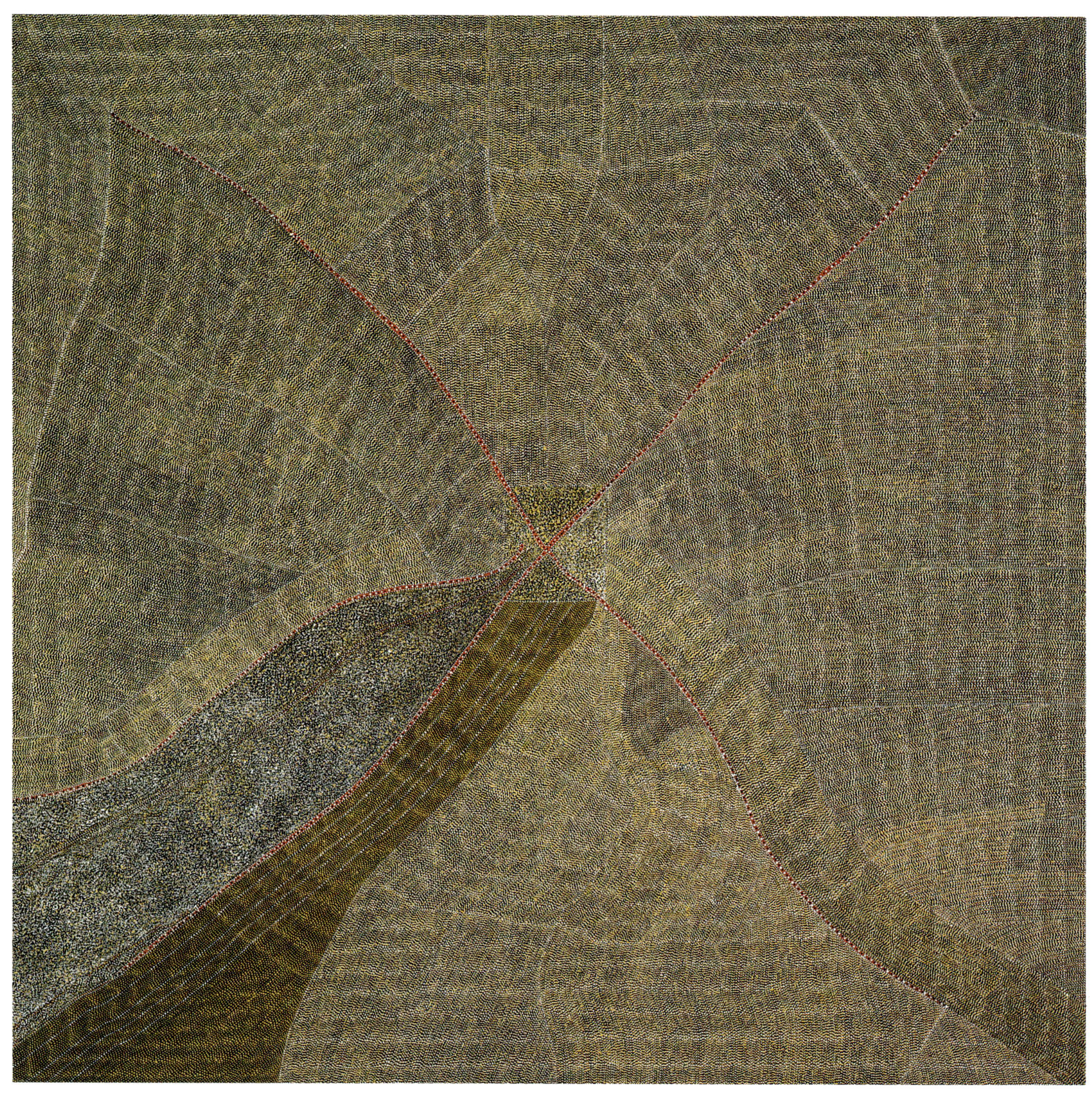

Mountain Devil Lizard Dreaming 1997 Synthetic polymer paint on Belgian linen 182.5 x 182. 5 cm (6' x 6') Private collection, Brisbane, Australia. Exhibited 27 November 1998, Seppelt Contemporary Art Award, Museum of Contemporary Art, Sydney

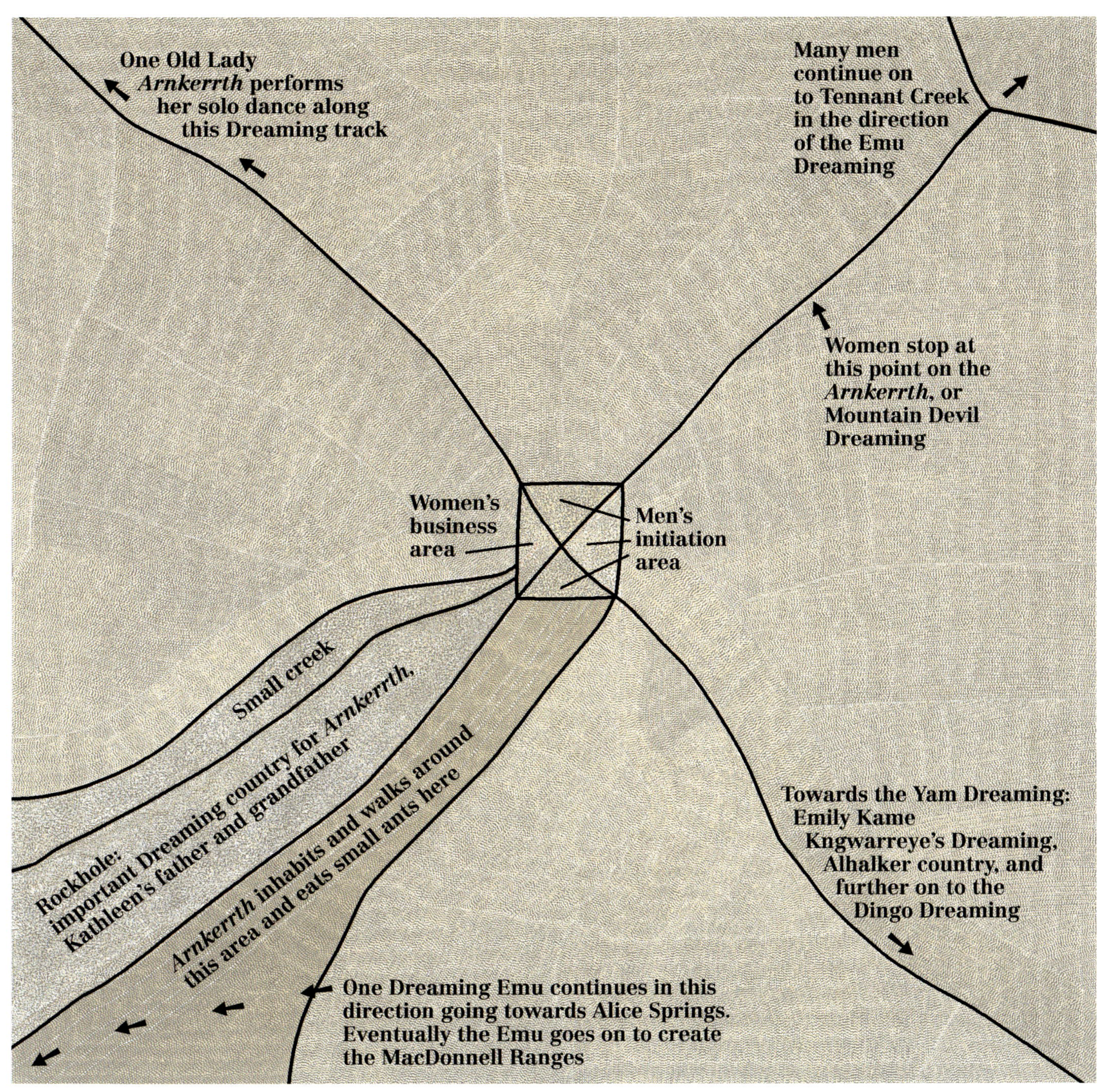

Diagram showing significant sites in Kathleen Petyarre's *Mountain Devil Lizard Dreaming 1997.* Diagram courtesy Kathleen Petyarre, Christine Nicholls and Maggie Fletcher, Flinders University Art Museum, South Australia

By this stage, the federal government's Assimilation Policy had achieved quasi-official status, although it was not officially adopted until 1952. The assimilationist era, during which Kathleen Petyarre was growing up, could be described as one of ethno-linguistic cleansing in intent, if not always in practice. Fortunately however, owing to their remote location, Petyarre and other Anmatyerr people were less directly affected by such policies and ideas than many other Indigenous Australian groups.

Several years after first meeting a white man, while still a teenager, Kathleen married a much older Anmatyerr man, to whom she had been 'promised' as a young child:

My mother-in-law chose me as wife for her son, to give to her son, when he had his [young man's initiation] ceremony. I was promised to that husband, but I ran away, I went back to stop with my mother all the time. Me and Violet were married to the same man, but Violet stayed with that same man after I ran away. I stopped with him about ten years maybe.

During these years, from her late teens to her late twenties, Kathleen attempted to conform to what it meant to be a 'traditional' Anmatyerr wife and mother, and gave birth to her only child, daughter Margaret Pwerle. Over that decade, she devoted herself to family and ceremonial responsibilities, but was becoming increasingly restless.

In 1968 the Northern Territory Department of Education, the official name of which was, at that stage, the Education Branch (Northern Territory) of the Welfare Branch/Division, announced that at the beginning of the following year it would be opening a small western-style school for the children of Utopia, and that a local person would be employed to work alongside the first white teaching staff as the teaching assistant. Kathleen jumped at the chance, immediately putting her name forward for the job, and winning the position. Strong-willed, clear-headed and focused in terms of her personal aspirations, Petyarre was seeking a dimension to her life that went beyond being a young wife and mother.

Working in Utopia School, 1969–1988

After leaving her husband, Kathleen made what would prove to be one of the most important decisions of her life. In 1969 she began working in the Utopia School, which opened in the same year.

'Utopia' is the umbrella name describing more than 20 small Aboriginal communities on the homelands of the Eastern Anmatyerr and Alyawarr speaking peoples of the Northern Territory. Theoretically, all children living in those small communities were eligible to enrol in the central school, in which Kathleen continued to work as an assistant teacher for 20 years. Because of lack of transportation, however, many children in the district could not actually attend with any regularity (see Richardson 2001, for more on this).

The school itself was a caravan of the type known as a 'silver bullet' in Northern Territory parlance. Inside, it was boiling in summer and freezing in winter. There was no air-conditioning or cooling in the caravan, and even the water supply was unreliable. The working conditions were appalling. Kathleen perceived her role as one of acting as cultural mediator between the Anmatyerr/Alyawarr community and the white teachers. At the same time, she herself was learning the dominant culture and language.

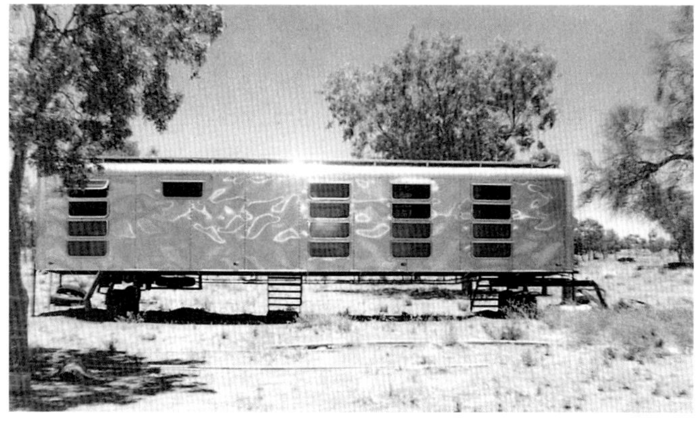

Utopia School caravan classroom where Kathleen Petyarre worked from 1969 to 1989 Photograph courtesy Frank and Anne Brennan

Kathleen's was a challenging position, because on the one hand most members of the local Anmatyerr and Alyawarr community had little or no idea of the purposes and processes of western schooling, and for that reason, had very good reason to be suspicious of it. Unlike Kathleen, most people did not readily embrace the imposed new order. On the other hand, almost all the young white teachers who staffed the school were newly arrived 'out bush', with little or no knowledge of Anmatyerr language or history, let alone the subtleties of inter-cultural communication.[2]

During her years of service Kathleen was the only continuous Anmatyerr adult presence in the Utopia school, providing a link between the wider Anmatyerr community and the passing parade of mostly neophyte teachers. Some teachers stayed for less than a year, some valued Kathleen and her contribution to education in the community and some clearly did not appreciate what she had to offer. Kathleen Petyarre recalls all of the teachers with extraordinary clarity:

I started working in the school with Mr and Mrs Brennan and also Miss O'Connor. Mr Brennan is a good man – it's Mr and Mrs Brennan's baby that I'm holding in that photo . . . Mr Brennan didn't hit the kids. Mrs Brennan learned us sewing. . . . In Mr Brennan-time, all the Anmatyerr ladies came up to the school and we made uniforms for the boys and girls with the words 'Utopia School' on it for all the kids, red writing, red uniforms.

We made the uniforms in a very big classroom. We had two sewing machines to make the uniforms, in the big classroom. Kids would have shower first, then into uniforms. Every day the kids would wear their uniforms, they had to put them on in the classrooms, they were told to put them on in the classrooms, and then take them off when they went home. Violet [Kathleen's sister] would wash them – Violet worked in the laundry. I was teaching Anmatyerr language – I was just talking story one day to Mr Brennan – then after that I worked in the school – I was talking lingo [Anmatyerr language] in the school – the kids understood me.

Over the years much of what Kathleen did in the school went well beyond any conventional duty statement for assistant teachers. In early 1969 flooding cut the road to Utopia. Teacher Anne Brennan, lacking fresh food and protein in her diet, experienced difficulty breast-feeding her baby Kirstin. Kathleen came up with a solution. Frank Brennan, Anne's husband and the other teacher at Utopia School, vividly remembers that difficult time:

We were very concerned that Kirstin – three months old I think – didn't seem to be gaining weight. You need to know the context of this: no doctor except in Alice Springs, and only the survey sisters to do health checks in the camp ever ten weeks or so. Annie, a 21-year-old first time mother, me a more-than-useless 24-year-old, decided to ask Kathleen what to do. Kathleen said to Annie, 'Show me titties.' Annie immediately lowered the top of her dress. Kathleen examined her, then pronounced, 'Ahhh tut, tut, tut. No milk. You giv'em bottle.' So Annie did, and baby Kirstin thrived. She is now teaching in Darwin and running marathons. Kathleen really saved Kirstin's life and our sanity.

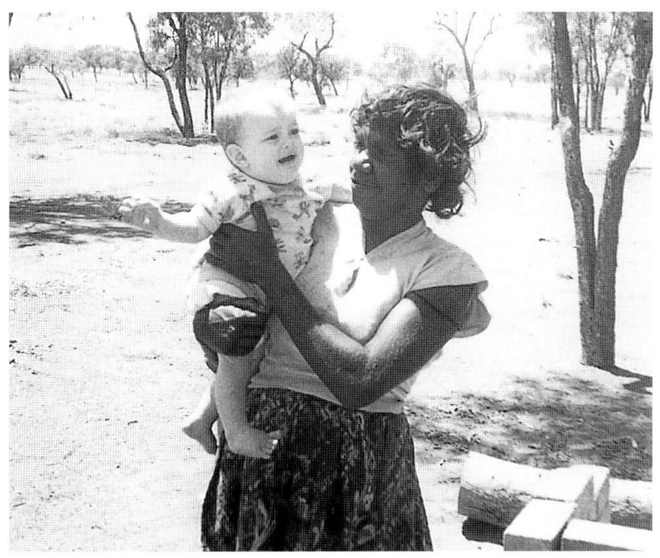

Kathleen Petyarre nursing baby Kirstin Brennan, the school teachers' daughter, Utopia, 1969 Photograph courtesy Frank and Anne Brennan

After that Kathleen felt responsible for Kirstin, often walking around with the baby on her arm, and sometimes feeding the Brennans' baby herself.

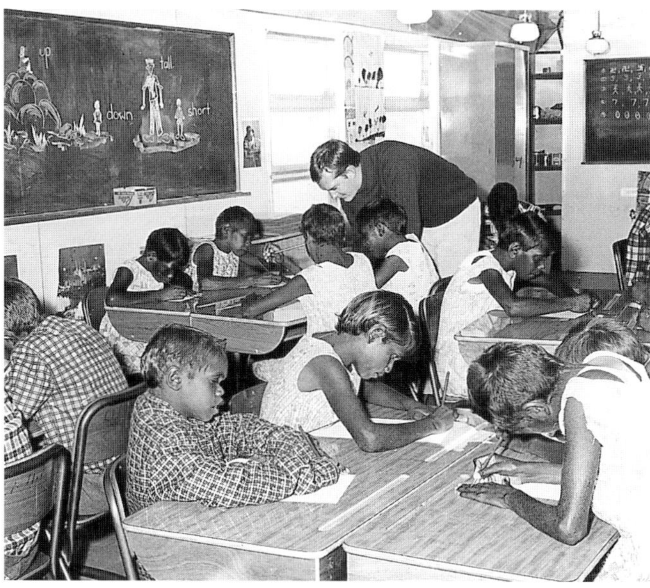

Utopia School caravan classroom, January 1969. The students shown include Bob Long Kngwarreye, Jeannie Petyarre, Paddy Clark Petyarre and Stevie Loy Kemarre. The teacher is Frank Brennan Photograph courtesy Frank and Anne Brennan

During her years of teaching in the school Kathleen Petyarre accompanied a number of the white teachers on excursions to other parts of the Territory and interstate. She has always been passionate about travel and loved this aspect of her job. During one of those excursions (c. 1974), when a Mrs Martins was the teacher at Utopia School, Kathleen and her countrywomen visited Canberra, Sydney and Wollongong in New South Wales. For Kathleen, the highlight of the trip was a visit to a hippy commune where batik T-shirts were being made:

Mrs Martins started showing us a little bit of batik first. We went down to Wollongong with Mrs Martins, and visited a place and saw some people doing batik in Wollongong. They were doing T-shirt. That the first time we ever heard about batik. Big place in Wollongong, they were making batik T-shirts on the ground. Whitefella like hippy. Rosemary [Petyarre] was chosen to mix up the colours, and they took pictures of us, those whitefellas. Violet did a bit of batik there. All the children took one of the batik T-shirts home. All of the children from Mulga Bore went, we mixed them all up. Then all the kids went swimming in the sea at Wollongong.[3]

For the most part, Kathleen performed what superficially seemed to be rather menial tasks in the school, while in fact undertaking an extraordinarily difficult and challenging intercultural balancing act. Her experience in cross-cultural education proved to be one of her most valuable assets when later she set about establishing an artistic career.

While Petyarre was working at the Utopia School, an astonishing renaissance of Indigenous artistic production began taking place in Central and Northern Australia, in places where the practice of making Indigenous art had survived colonisation. Artistic practices including body painting, ground painting and the creation and decoration of ceremonial objects using ochres and other natural media, grounded in Indigenous religion, had continued with (mostly) only minor disruption in remote locations like the Anmatyerr homelands. But often people paid a heavy price for such artistic and cultural maintenance. Frequently Indigenous art practice had been forced 'underground' as it were, practised covertly, sometimes late at night, away from the watchful gaze of the missionaries or the surveillance of government authorities.

It was during the assimilationist era that many, but not all, of the Central Australian and Western Desert Aboriginal settlements were established. In 1971, when the Australian government was on the cusp of changing its policy towards Indigenous Australians in the direction of self-determination, a young art teacher, Geoffrey Bardon, arrived at Papunya School (see map). Bardon was receptive to the Aboriginal community's desire for self-determination and showed a willingness to act as a catalyst for change. A group of men who interacted closely with him created a mural of their traditional designs or

Dreamings on a 10 x 3 metre wall of the Papunya School. This not only brightened up the school, but constituted a strong, collective assertion of the importance of Aboriginal culture. The mural was provocatively positioned fair and square in the middle of the white man's school, which was quite accurately regarded as a bastion of the assimilation project. Among those original mural painters were the legendary Old Masters Kaapa Mbitjana (Tjampitjinpa), Long Jack Phillipus and Billy Stockman Tjapaltjarri.

Soon after this highly symbolic action (later to be painted over, literally and metaphorically whitewashed, by the Northern Territory Department of Education) the now famous Papunya Tula Artists' cooperative was established. Papunya Tula Artists Pty Ltd came into being in 1972 as a collective owned and controlled by artists and members of the predominantly Pintupi community at Papunya, and continues to thrive today.

The momentous events at Papunya gave rise to what could be described as a genuine revolution in the marketing and ultimately in the status of Indigenous Australian art. First Papunya art was launched onto the national stage, then in the international arena. Its most important social spin-off has been its impact on other Aboriginal communities in the Northern Territory. Soon other Indigenous Australian communities began to emulate the success of Papunya. What started as a small community ripple grew into a tidal wave.

Utopia followed Papunya's example, eventually becoming one of the most important art-producing communities. What differentiates Utopia from almost all of the other contemporary Indigenous art movements is the fact that from its inception the overwhelming majority of practitioners have been women. This came about as a result of a fortuitous synchronicity, where the Indigenous art renaissance movement became entangled with a social movement that was gaining momentum in Australia and elsewhere in the Western world: second-wave feminism. At the time, second-wave feminism in Australia was by and large limited to white, middle-class women. In the late 1970s one such young woman went to live in Utopia.

Kathleen Petyarre and the Utopia Batik Movement, 1977-1986

When Jenny Green arrived in Utopia in 1977 and began work as a part-time adult education instructor for the Northern Territory Education Department, she organised workshops in batik method. The women who had travelled to Wollongong already had a rudimentary grasp of the process and its intended outcome. At first, Jenny Green taught tie-dyeing and wood block printing:

Jenny Green taught us tie-dyeing with a rock – put different colours, yellow first, orange and red, blue, yellow –she taught us to tie-dye. Jenny Green came and started teaching all the myall [Aboriginal English for 'ignorant' or 'unschooled'] people – they never learned [before that time]. All the ladies mostly – one [was] Aunty Emily [Emily Kame Kngwarreye]. All the young girls and middle-aged women like us. I still kept going in the school, but when I knock[ed] off at the end of the day, that time I do batik. When Violet finish her work in the laundry, then she would do batik. Making good money from selling batik – proper money. [Violet adds: Three hundred and four hundred – good money!]

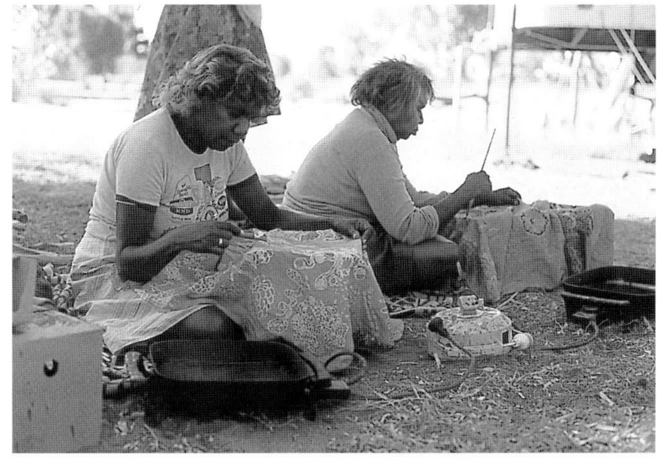

Hilda Pwerle (left) and Kathleen Petyarre making batik, Utopia, late 1970s Photograph courtesy Jenny Green

Kathleen Petyarre and her younger sister Gloria Petyarre were among the sizeable group of Alyawarr and Eastern Anmatyerr women of Utopia who began learning the techniques of batik and screen printing in the late 1970s. The late Emily Kame Kngwarreye emerged as an artist from their ranks when she was already in her late seventies. Kngwarreye took the Australian and international art world by storm, an amazing feat for one who was not only positioned at the extreme margins of the dominant Australian culture, but was also so advanced in years.

These and many other women enthusiastically embraced the adult education program conducted first by Jenny Green, and in later years, by Julia Murray and others. Green has written about this era, saying that:

. . . there is no doubt that for many of these artists, batik was the first major innovation which provided the creative link between the traditional and the contemporary. Batik was immediately popular for its recreational as well as its economic potential, and the Utopia women took to it with characteristic energy and enthusiasm. Batik is hard work – the process of applying wax to cloth (or row upon row of acrylic dots to canvas) requires some of the patience, dexterity and determination employed in winnowing seed or collecting other bushtuckers. In modern times Utopia women alternate between these activities with ease, and the production of artwork has become an important part of the economic life of bush communities in Central Australia.

The Utopia women have developed a style which is distinctive for its spontaneity and boldness of gesture. The intricate batik designs captured on silk and other fabrics by these artists tell stories of the traditional lands on which the majority of them continue to live. The symbolism in the batik, like everything else, is ultimately derived from the Altyerr ['The Dreaming'] – the creative principle which saturates the world with meaning. (Green 1998:38)

Kathleen Petyarre worked extremely hard through the batik years. Not only was she committed to her work at the Utopia School with Toly Sawenko, with whom she really enjoyed team teaching, but she also took on a political battle of far-reaching magnitude, becoming involved in a land claim of immense significance to the Anmatyerr. Kathleen was a key claimant for Anmatyerr Freehold Title over the Utopia Pastoral Lease, which had been purchased for the community in 1976 by the Commonwealth Aboriginal Land Fund Commission. She was *kwertengerl* for the land claim over Atetyerr, the land belonging to her mother and other relations on her mother's side. The claim eventually proved successful and in 1980 the land around Utopia was formally returned to its traditional owners. Like many other Indigenous Australians, Kathleen Petyarre has consistently emphasised the strong connection between her land and her art. Each of her batiks and canvases is an assertion of land rights, an expression of her inalienable connection with Atnangker country and its associated Dreaming, *Arnkerrth*.

The 'batik era' was an important one for Kathleen Petyarre, both personally and professionally. Historically, it will almost certainly be recognised as a significant social movement. It represented a small but important step in the direction of economic self-determination and self-sufficiency for the Utopia women, as well as a collective expression of the politics of land rights. The group of women involved in the batik movement collectively constitute a distinct group whose artistic work, in terms of the national imaginary, is as important as that of the Heidelberg School.

In the early days, however, marketing the batik was hard work. There was a constant need to create and massage markets, and a sense of continually going against the grain in terms of the prevailing racism and sexism of those times. Jenny Green notes that:

Initially markets for Utopia batik were developed slowly, with work being sold at the first exhibition held at Mona Byrne's gallery in Alice Springs. Other connections in Sydney and in various small outlets in Alice Springs resulted in more sales and commissions. Some batik was also sold to local staff of the

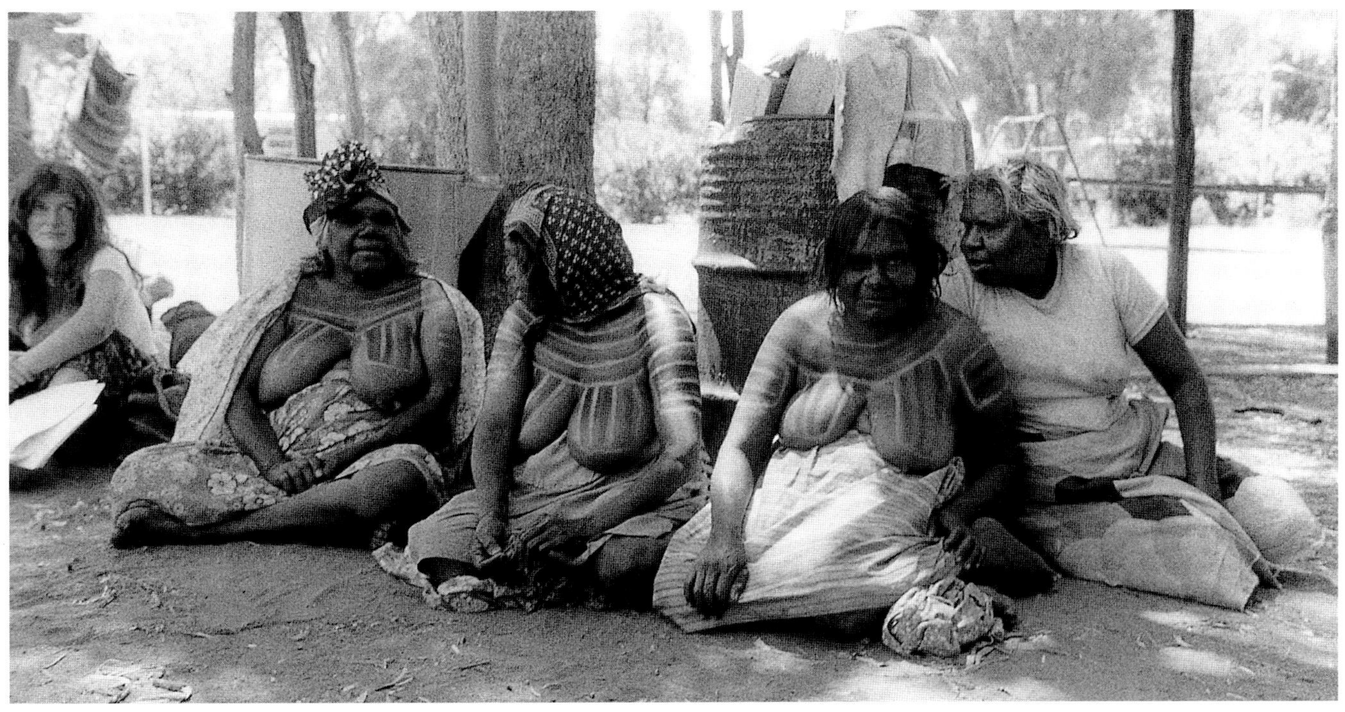

Above: Anmatyerr/Alyawarr Land Claim - Anmatyerr women painted for *awely*, late 1970s. From left: four sisters, Selina Pwerle, Eily Pwerle, Ada Pwerle and Gladdy Pwerle Photograph courtesy Diane Bell

Below: Justice Toohey hearing the Anmatyerr Land Claim, late 1970s. From left: Norah Kemarre, Bunny Kemarre, Polly Pwerle, Emily Kngwarreye and Justice Toohey Photograph courtesy Diane Bell

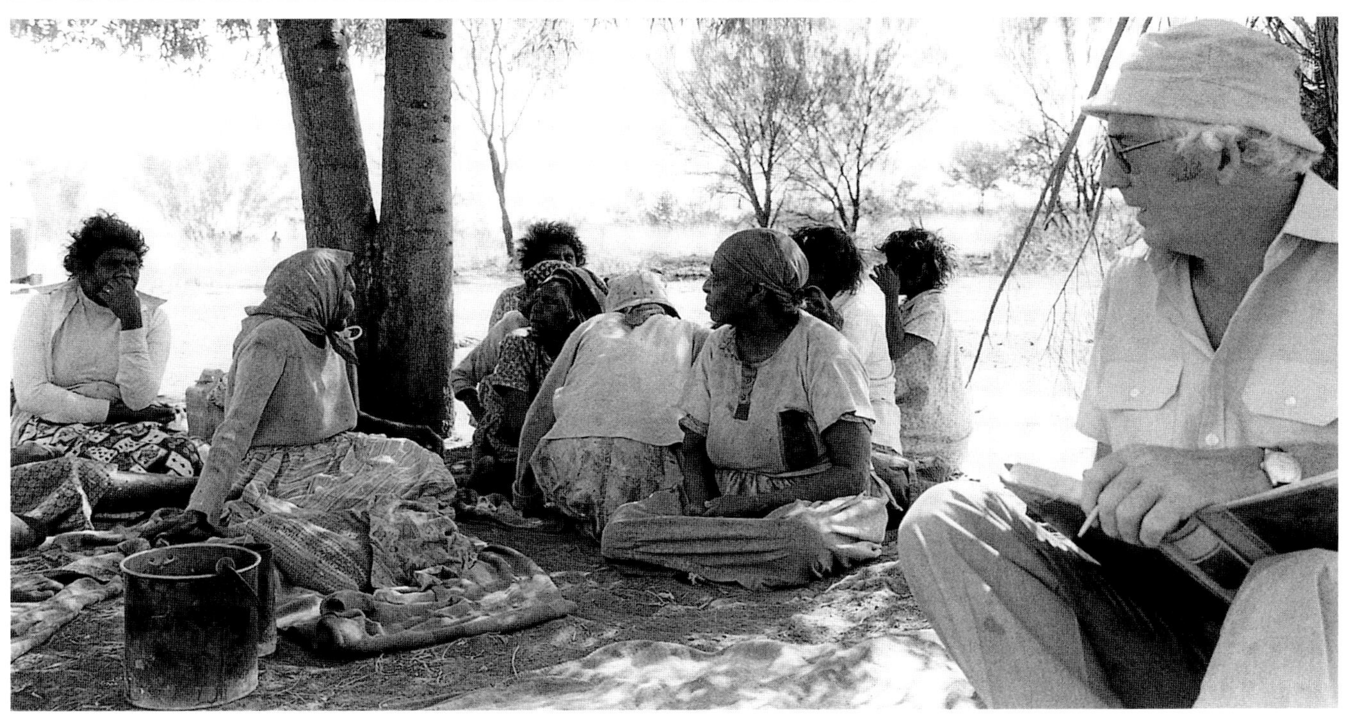

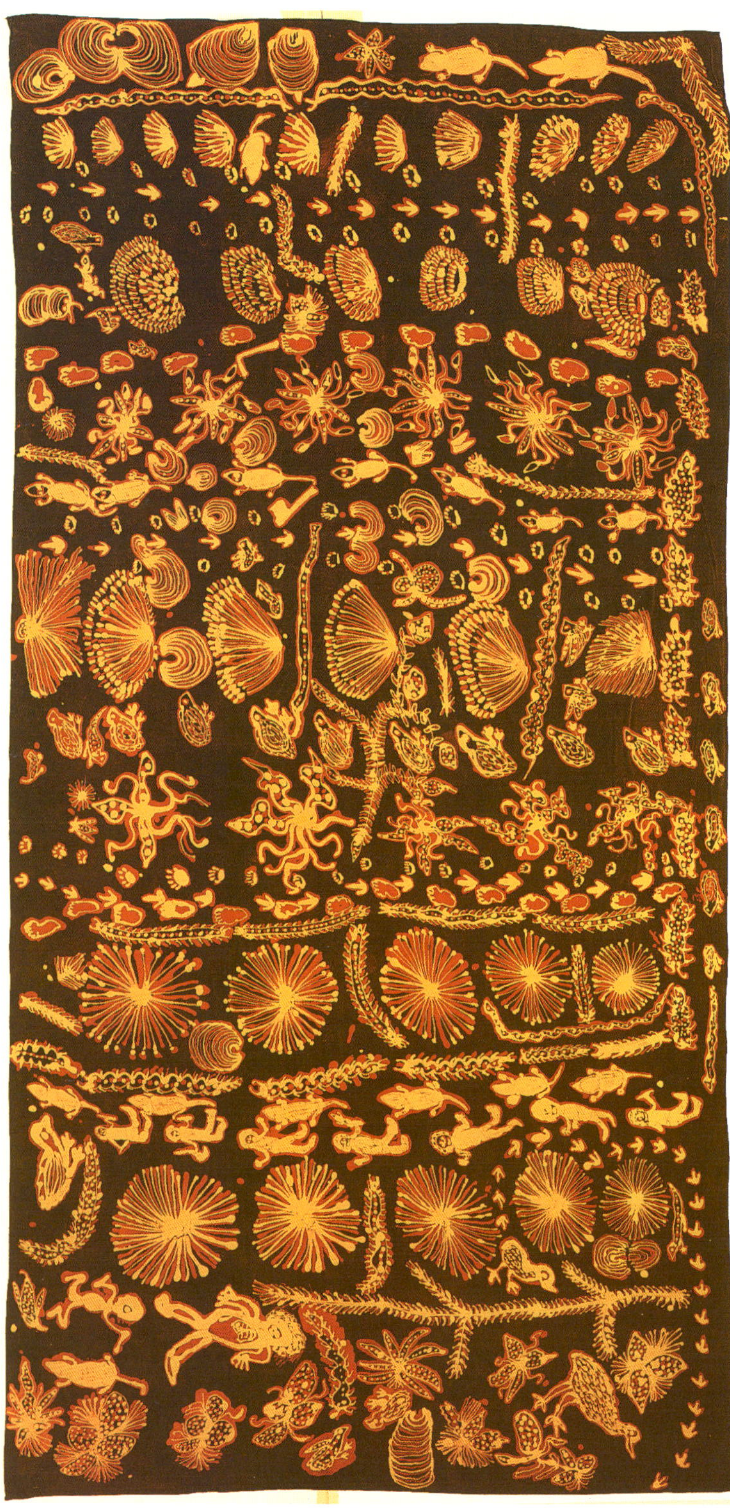

Atnangkere Story, Kathleen Petyarre, Utopia 1988, batik on silk, 232 x 118 cm
The Holmes à Court Collection, Heytesbury, Western Australia

Urapuntja Health Service, interested schoolteachers and other staff from the Utopia community, visitors and passing tourists. There were, on occasion, even batik 'lawn sales' in Alice Springs. Later, exhibitions were held at the Araluen Art Centre in Alice Springs and at various other venues, both local and interstate. Such markets depended on local connections and hard work . . . as they probably still do, although in later years the work of the Utopia women achieved significant national and international prominence.

In the early days there was little recognition of Aboriginal women's work as 'art' and work on fabric was a new medium that likewise was little known. Consequently the prices were low in comparison to those of today, and also low in comparison to the prices commanded by the Papunya artists who were working on canvas.

The money generated from the sale of the batik had an important symbolic value because the women earned it themselves, and it was one of the few opportunities the women had to generate supplementary income. They appreciated the opportunity to display their work and the obvious enthusiasm it generated from an appreciative audience.

Batik was the first experiment in non-traditional art media.

In the beginning the women did not incorporate awely designs into their batik, or at least this was not a common theme of their work. This first happened in the 1980s, and it is hard to say whether this was a strategic decision on the part of the women to reveal more of their particular ceremonial business, or just a development of the possibilities of batik, and later of the painting media. This is not to deny that there has been increasing pressure on all Aboriginal artists from the 'art market' to reveal the cultural content of their artwork, and this has had a huge effect on the development of this art.

In an indirect way I suppose the white women who worked for the Utopia mob had a fundamental belief in social justice, and the importance of women's rights at all levels, and this belief grew out of the popular social movements and the consciousness of

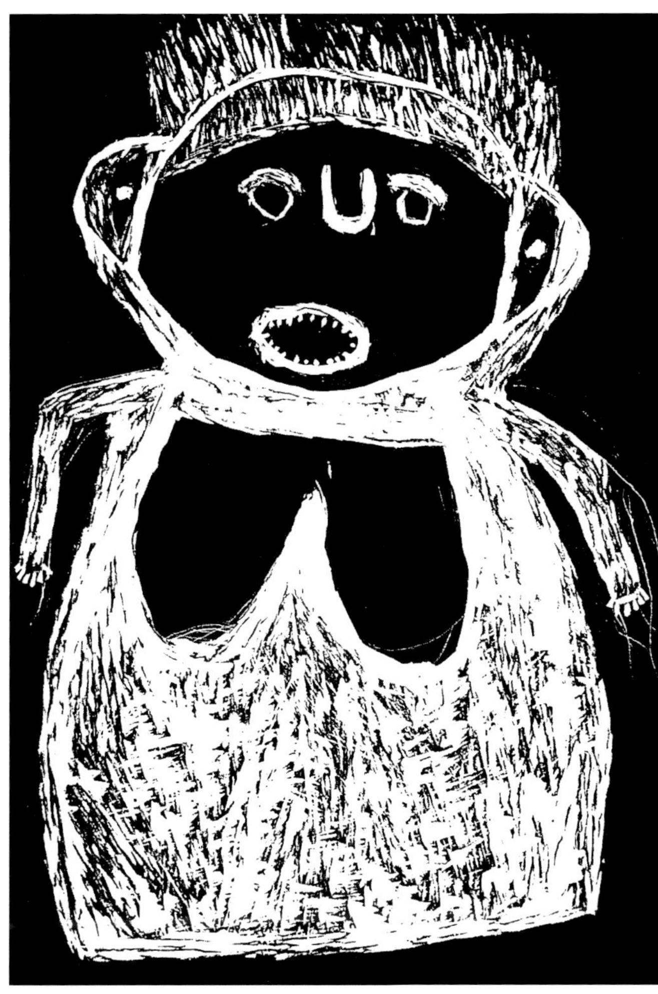

Kathleen Petyarre, Untitled 1990 (from Utopia print series), Woodcut, 45 x 30 cm (image size), 52.2 x 37.6 cm (paper size), Edition No. 2/20 Photograph and image courtesy Christopher Hodges, Utopia Art Sydney

the time. In the context of emerging bureaucracies and organisations that were in part the interface between black and white cultures in the Northern Territory, this meant supporting women's initiatives, both economic and cultural. The drive for artistic and economic independence was part of this. One outcome is that the production of art has certainly become a career for some of the women. (9 April 2001).

The fact that this social movement was driven by a group of Anmatyerr and Alyawarr *women* strongly asserting the land/identity nexus challenged the norms and practices that had perpetuated inequality and discrimination in this country, after European arrival, is also significant. The model of Indigenous women working with a succession of white women of considerable vision, the first of whom set up a viable infrastructure for what would become a cottage industry, may be read as a way forward for Indigenous and non-Indigenous reconciliation, before 'Reconciliation' was mooted as a formal process.

But the batik movement represented more than a symbolic blow against racism and sexism. The fact that the women's efforts were honoured and recognised in the wider social arena gave many of that early group of batik artists, including Kathleen Petyarre, the skills and the confidence to further their artistic careers.

From Batik to Acrylics on Canvas, 1986-1992

As the years went by, Petyarre's allergy to the fumes produced by the strong chemicals used in batik-production became intolerable:

All the ladies were doing batik with Jenny Green. I was doing batik first but I didn't like it because of the smoke, the wax and the smell. So I was happy to finish doing it, because it made me asthma, my chest and breathing was bad because of smell.

Kathleen had begun to perceive batik as a tedious process as well as a danger to her health – perhaps it was no longer worth the trouble. When in 1986 a new art adviser, Rodney Gooch, arrived in Utopia, Kathleen readily took up his suggestion of painting with acrylics on canvas, in the wake of the extraordinary success of other Central Australian painting communities.

Gooch remained at Utopia as art adviser until 1992. During his years there he organised numerous exhibitions of the artists' work, and was successful in pushing their sales as well as their public profile. By the early 1990s the Utopia artists were firmly on the cultural map, supported by an adventitious succession of capable and professional art advisers.

Kathleen cites Rodney Gooch as one of the people who has been most influential in terms of her career as an artist, and she is still very fond of him: 'Rodney still works at Alice Springs . . . every time he sees me he gives me a big hug and says "Ohhh Kathleen!" Every time he sees me!'

For his own part, when Rodney Gooch first arrived at Utopia, he found Kathleen to be the most forthcoming and approachable of all of the women artists. He appreciated Petyarre's wicked sense of humour, extroverted nature, and drive to succeed. Given Kathleen's status as a fine artist these days, it is interesting to note that Gooch considered Petyarre's early acrylics on canvas to be 'rather awkward in terms of their execution – initially, they didn't seem to work, entirely'. In Gooch's opinion, Kathleen took a considerable time to come to terms with the new medium. From today's perspective, Petyarre's early acrylics on canvas are competent but unremarkable 'dot and circle' works betraying strongly the stylistic influence of the Papunya school, which by that time had become hugely popular and in great demand.

In 1991 Kathleen met Welsh-born itinerant labourer Ray Beamish in Alice Springs. Eventually Petyarre and Beamish became a couple, and Beamish, who is many years Kathleen's junior, moved to Utopia as Kathleen's de facto husband. Beamish made himself useful and developed a limited profile around Utopia by occasionally helping some of the old men add dots to their paintings, an activity that many found time-consuming and boring.

In terms of Anmatyerr law, dots are the least significant aspect of the painting, often, though not always, thought of simply as infill. Collaboration with others, while rule-bound, is simply 'business as usual' for Centralian and Western Desert Indigenous artists, and performed openly in virtually all of the art-producing communities.

Kathleen Petyarre is an erudite, family-oriented Anmatyerr woman, deeply immersed in Anmatyerr Law and in her Dreaming, and a pillar of her community. Ray Beamish is a dreamer and drifter with a passion for big motorbikes. From the beginning their relationship seemed ill-fated to some observers. Rodney Gooch, for example 'had a bad feeling about that relationship right from the start'.

After assisting the old men for some time with their paintings, Beamish assisted Petyarre by applying dots to some of her canvases from time to time, in a manner consistent with Anmatyerr Law – that is, always under her control and direction. Kathleen Petyarre summarises her custodial rights in the following terms:

Mountain Devil [Arnkerrth], Bush Seeds [Ntang] and Green Bean [Nyterrm] – you know the one – are my true Dreamings. No whitefella can paint [those] Dreamings under Anmatyerr Law – there's no problem if I tell them to put some dots on Mountain Devil, Bush Seeds or Bean Dreaming, but only dots and only when I tell them. I'm not allowed to paint other [Anmatyerr] people's Dreaming either – I've just got to do my own Dreaming. Otherwise big trouble – our Law says, 'Not allowed!' Doing wrong Dreaming (someone else Dreaming) – that would make big trouble for me, big problem.

Towards the end of Rodney Gooch's stay at Utopia, Kathleen Petyarre's dream of being recognised as a great artist became more focused. She wished to succeed her Aunt Emily Kame Kngwarreye as the most feted Anmatyerr artist. As a result, Petyarre began tailoring her paintings to suit her own 'reading' of the demands of non-Indigenous art markets:

I wanted to be famous artist – when middle-aged woman – [I wanted] all the ladies and children following me, like Aunty Emily mob. So I really tried hard to do the painting the way whitefellas like it – they like neat one, and now I don't do quick one, I do it slow. Those who do quick one only get 'quick one money'! I do 'im slow, and all the time put little dots, sometimes I do dots two weeks, three weeks, on my canvas. The whitefella like that one, that way.

It says a good deal about Kathleen Petyarre's highly developed cross-cultural facility and skills that she was able to gauge with such accuracy the mood and desires of the mostly metropolitan-based art markets while based in Utopia, a remote community by any standards.

By 1992 Kathleen and Ray had travelled to South Australia and the couple were living intermittently with Beamish's mother south of Adelaide. Petyarre was however going back to Utopia regularly to spend time with her family.

During that summer Kathleen and Ray started canvassing Adelaide's art galleries on foot, looking for a gallery dealer to act on Kathleen's behalf. Having no luck at Tandanya, Adelaide's principal Indigenous cultural centre, and after being turned away from galleries elsewhere, Kathleen and Ray eventually cruised into Gallerie Australis, owned by David Cossey and managed by Penelope Hoile. Situated on North Terrace, Adelaide, at the base of the Hyatt Hotel, Gallerie Australis caters to the fine-art market Australia-wide and internationally.

Initially David Cossey was not overwhelmingly impressed by Kathleen's work but he saw genuine potential in her developing style. Although her relatively early acrylic works are characterised by a high level of care and attention to detail, one can see only fleeting glimpses of Petyarre's elegant, finely wrought, lyrical compositions of later years. But Cossey came to the conclusion that such talent should be nurtured and he commissioned Petyarre to paint several works, supplying her with paints and canvas. He stipulated that the paintings should look as similar as possible to one of Kathleen's earlier works that he had seen reproduced in the Holmes à Court Collection catalogue.

That first meeting was a turning point in Kathleen Petyarre's artistic career. It led to a long, amicable and productive collaboration between Kathleen as an artist and David Cossey as her agent. Their continuing business relationship, which entails a close personal friendship based on mutual regard, continues to this day. In 1995 Kathleen signed a contract giving Gallerie Australis exclusive rights of representation of her work.

Following that first serendipitous meeting with David Cossey, Kathleen's career progressed quietly and steadily (at first). In 1996 her first solo exhibition, *Kathleen Petyarre – Storm in Aknangkere*[4] *Country*, opened at the up-market Alcaston House Gallery, in Spring Street, Melbourne. The show was a sell-out, which represented a phenomenal success given that Petyarre was virtually an unknown artist at the time.

While Kathleen herself and David Cossey had carefully laid the groundwork for such success, the Melbourne exhibition introduced her work to a wider audience. After that Petyarre's career took off exponentially, and her work is now represented in major collections throughout the world. Kathleen Petyarre's rising profile as an artist in the late 1990s also offered her many opportunities for interstate travel, and for seeing the world.

Storm in Atnangkere Country II: the Row Over the 1996 Telstra Art Award

Ray – what you thinking of for me . . . what for you humbugging me? . . . I'm sorry for you Ray. You bin pinch 'im my Dreaming. Now I'm not talking to any more television or newspaperman or woman. I can talk through lawyer man from now on.

In 1996 Kathleen Petyarre was announced as the overall winner of the 13th Telstra National Aboriginal & Torres Strait Islander Art Award, the longest-running, most lucrative and most prestigious Indigenous art prize in the country. Winning the prize – for her magisterial work *Storm in Atnangkere Country II* – brought Kathleen the longed-for fame, but it also led to unwelcome media attention.

In late 1997, Ray Beamish, who by this time had left Kathleen, incited a scandal in the Australian art world by 'confessing' to an art critic working for the *Australian* newspaper that he, and not Kathleen Petyarre, had painted the lion's share of the prize-winning entry. The media 'case' against Petyarre hinged, *inter alia*, on the putative 'confessions' that the *Australian* journalist had obtained from not only

Beamish but also apparently from Kathleen Petyarre herself, regarding the authorship of the work. 'Lauded black artist confesses, it's not my work', announced the newspaper on 23 December 1997.

In addition, some faint-hearted art gallery curators began prematurely altering the signage on paintings formerly attributed to Kathleen Petyarre, by adding the name 'Ray Beamish' to Kathleen's, prior to the resolution of the formal investigation into the media allegations. Many people, it seemed, had something to say something about this business. Knowing little about the epistemological foundations of Anmatyerr artistic production did not seem to stop some commentators having their say.

It is worth briefly discussing the significance of the notion of a 'confession' of wrongdoing in terms of what it might mean from the perspective of a speaker of an Indigenous language, like Kathleen Petyarre, who also speaks Aboriginal English. For Kathleen, English is a third, not even a second language. Petyarre's spoken English is limited in repertoire and heavily accented. This often makes it difficult for non-speakers of Indigenous Australian languages to comprehend. The reverse is also the case – Kathleen has difficulty understanding unfamiliar English syntax, in particular. When English speakers use unfamiliar grammatical constructions, lexical items or questioning techniques (the pragmatics of which are quite different in her own language, in which direct questioning is unusual and regarded as extraordinarily invasive) Petyarre often does not understand the intent of the question, and has a tendency to agree with whatever proposition is being floated. Equally, the notion of a 'confession' has strongly Christian overtones. There is no exactly equivalent word or concept for the idea of a 'confession' in any Australian Indigenous language.

This phenomenon, which is by no means confined to Kathleen Petyarre, but is well documented in Australianist linguistics and sociolinguistics, has been glossed as 'gratuitous concurrence'[5] and is widely held to be a feature of the Aboriginal linguistic repertoire, both 'traditional' (pre-contact) and contemporary.

Several commentators, notably Djon Mundine, Avril Quaill, and Doreen Mellor, made sensible and lucid statements on the issue, but their commentaries did not receive the same oxygen of publicity as the detractors. Art critic Joanna Mendelssohn, in an Opinion piece in the *Australian* (24/12/97) was among the very few voices who demonstrated an informed understanding of the issues and what was really at stake for Indigenous artists in such circumstances. Importantly, Mendelssohn distinguished between what had happened in the case of Kathleen Petyarre and Beamish, and real cultural imposture, such as white artist Elizabeth Durack's extended cyber-masquerade as a pretend Aboriginal artist. Mendelssohn expertly cut to the chase when she wrote that:

It is a peculiar burden we lay on Aboriginal culture, to be authentic in both the Western and Aboriginal sense. We expect Aboriginal art to be true to itself in terms of understanding, to keep the meanings of the stories (which most westerners don't know) and to look the way we expect it to look . . . In this case, the crime is that Petyarre was 'caught' behaving in a communal manner with the person with whom she was cohabiting. Forgive me if I am not shocked.

There was also a gender issue in this affair. It seems that people are more readily disposed to accept that male Indigenous artists might legitimately be assisted in creating art works by women in their family (for example their wives and or daughters – the famous artist Michael Nelson Tjakamarra is one such case in point) but less prepared to accept Indigenous women artists being helped by their husbands or partners. When the partner also happens to be non-Indigenous, this adds another level of complexity to the public reception of such practices.

In 1997–1998 the Board of the Museum and Art Gallery of the Northern Territory conducted an inquiry into Beamish's (and the media's) allegations that he, and not Kathleen Petyarre, was the major contributor to the winning work. After several months of strenuous investigation, and many rounds of interviews, Colin McDonald QC, Chairman of the Board, announced on 24 April 1998 that:

. . . the Board found the allegations of Mr Beamish regarding the authorship of the painting were not proved. Accordingly, there is no basis for interfering with the decision of the judges awarding the 1996 Telstra Prize to Kathleen Petyarre. (24 April 1998)

The Chairman went on to note that while it was not in dispute that Ray Beamish had assisted with some of the dotting, ultimately this was not material to the decision in terms of what constituted authorship of the painting. Kathleen Petyarre's name was cleared and she was allowed to keep the prize money, but on a personal level, the entire sorry episode cost her dearly. Beamish's assertion of authorship plunged Petyarre into deep depression and at one point she felt that she never wished to paint again.

Because of the communal nature of the intellectual copyright asserted by Kathleen's extended family members over the Mountain Devil Dreaming, Beamish's claim upset not only Kathleen's but also some of her extended family and many other Anmatyerr people. In addition, Beamish had begun to paint solo works. Kathleen felt that Beamish had appropriated her birthright, that is, her Dreaming.

During this difficult time, which played itself out over almost eighteen months, a tight circle of family and friends supported Kathleen Petyarre financially and emotionally. Gallerie Australis stood by Petyarre during her bleakest days, engaging the Adelaide law firm Phillips Fox to assist in issuing statements outlining her position. Several other academics (including myself) and curators publicly defended the artist against the allegations.

In the end, Kathleen Petyarre refused to bow to the enormous pressure. She came back fighting; Petyarre's best work was yet to come. Part of the explanation for this is her genuine sense of vocation as an artist, which differentiates her from many other artists, both Indigenous and non-Indigenous. The other part relates to her early schooling in the *Arnkerrth* narrative. *Arnkerrth* is, after all, a survivor against the greatest odds. While Kathleen Petyarre bears the scars of a battle won, she goes on painting. Like *Arnkerrth*, she has arrived. Full circle.

Kathleen Petyarre, 1997–present

Like *Arnkerrth*, Kathleen Petyarre is a seasoned journey woman. Interstate and overseas travel is now a regular and integral part of Petyarre's schedule as an internationally renowned artist, and she loves this aspect of her life. Her most constant travelling companion is her sister Violet. These global excursions give Petyarre many opportunities to compare cultures:

I went to America [in 1998], me and Violet went there, and met up with a very big man [Richard Kelton of the Kelton Foundation in Los Angeles]. Richard Kelton's got a lot of paintings there, he collects them – yes, my Mountain Devil painting is there at the Foundation in Los Angeles. I've also been to Bali a while back with all my canvases – I had an exhibition there but I forget the name of the gallery [Museum Puri Lukasan, The King's Palace Museum, Ubud]. Good, nice people there in Bali, I like [the Balinese] better than Americans. Too much hugging and kissing in America! I've also been to England and Ireland and Scotland, India – that's it I think, always for my exhibitions.[6]

In November 1998 Kathleen, Violet and I, along with Adelaide-based Indigenous photographers Agnes Love and Polly Sumner, visited Los Angeles for the first time, as guests of the Kelton Foundation. While I found our cab rides along LA's 20-lane multi-levelled freeways quite terrifying the Petyarre sisters always remained unfazed, taking it all in their stride. Unlike me, they didn't seem to think that we were undergoing a near-death experience on the freeways, and were somewhat mystified by my lack of *sang-froid*.

In Los Angeles we were given a formidable sashimi lunch at the waterfront apartments of Richard Kelton, who owns one of the largest collections of Australian Aboriginal art in the world. Kathleen and Violet Petyarre viewed their Mountain

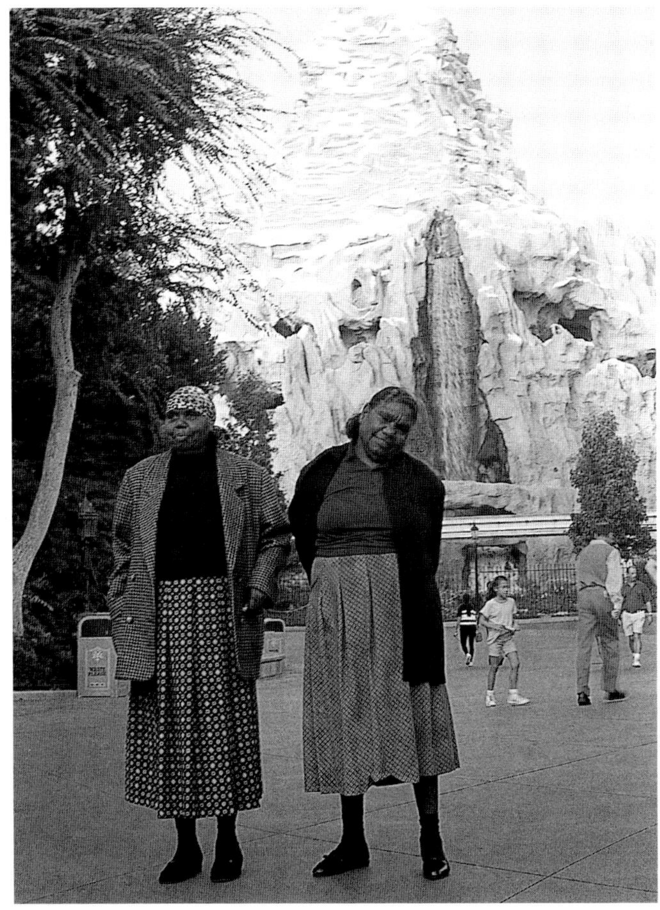

Violet Petyarre (left) and Kathleen Petyarre in Disneyland, California, United States of America, November 1998

Photograph courtesy Agnes Love

Devil paintings in the impressively large storage space housing the Kelton Collection, a context utterly different from their original place of creation.

Then we travelled to an international conference for Indigenous people held in Virginia Beach, Virginia, called 'Belonging to Mother Earth'. The conference was attended by Indigenous people from all over the world, many of whom were garbed in national or regional costumes. There were also numerous non-Indigenous delegates, ranging from interpreters and translators and others like myself, to philanthropists who were mainstream dressers, wealthy eccentrics wearing cheesecloth, baggy batiks, chains and crosses, and New-Agers sporting all manner of exotic attire. Many seemed to be seeking personal transfiguration via contact with 'authentic' Indigenous spirituality.

These days, Kathleen Petyarre occupies two worlds of status, at home and away, gliding apparently effortlessly (most of the time) across geographical and cultural space. As a result of her travels, Kathleen has had opportunities to observe many different artistic and cultural practices, and has formed some definite views. For example, she is scathing about contemporary post-modernism in art.

In September–October 2000 Kathleen, Violet and I were staying in Bali, near Ubud, on a working holiday. The sisters spent part of each day carefully observing the Balinese paddyfarmers working on the fields below their window. Kathleen said:

I like Bali painting, I like Bali art – I really like that one. I like Bali culture, up in the forest the people are little bit like Aboriginal people – they look little bit like Aboriginal people. What about that mob yesterday! Working in the rice – they built a little humpy for shade from hot sun, and sat under – they had a little kettle and boiled it. We watched them all day! They work, work, work every day they work, they work Sunday, never stop.

In April 2001 Kathleen Petyarre headed overseas again, on a visit organised by Adelaide's Tandanya Aboriginal Cultural Institute. This time she went to Rotorua in New Zealand as one of a group of Indigenous artists travelling to work on a collaborative artistic project with Maori artists. These days, international travel is pretty much 'business as usual' for Petyarre.

Her work and life exemplify a nascent, but growing, phenomenon that could be described as 'globalisation from below'. In terms of its production and reception both at home and elsewhere, Kathleen Petyarre's artistic practice challenges the received wisdom that globalisation is only ever imposed from 'above', by multinational corporations, superpowers and the like.

Congruent with such a position is Petyarre's incorporation of diverse styles and influences into her artistic *oeuvre*, and her rejection of others which she sees as lacking 'story'. At the same time her content remains fundamentally unchanged, despite the amplification of its possible meanings by processes of colonisation.

Like other Central Australian and Western Desert Indigenous artistic works, Kathleen Petyarre's representations of her Ancestor's travellings over Atnangker country act as a visual short-hand or abbreviated semiotic system standing for the much expanded, fuller *oral* narrative, which reveals in detail *Arnkerrth*'s heroic exploits during the Creation era known in inadequate English translation as 'The Dreaming'. This narrative can also be represented by a variety of other media – for example, it can be told, sung and danced. Indeed, Petyarre's controlled use of specific visual imagery to suggest *Arnkerrth*'s journeying, particularly her choice of a profusion of exquisite, tiny, radiating dots to represent *Arnkerrth*'s Lilliputian tracks, is evocative of certain kinds of music[7] and dance. Viewed from above, *Arnkerrth*'s tracks appear as a swirling, semicircular vortex of movement, as the Dreaming Ancestor makes her undulating progress through the Atnangker sand dunes and other natural obstructions.

Arnkerrth's circumambulations through the desert are hazardous not only physically but also psychologically. Like Ulysses and other epic travellers, *Arnkerrth* meets resistance from the forces of nature but sometimes also from other Beings she encounters during her travels. To survive, *Arnkerrth* must garner all of her considerable intellectual powers and strength; it is not simply a matter of forging ahead by brute force. The canniness that this implies is an important aspect of the oral version of the *Arnkerrth* Dreaming narrative, in which Petyarre portrays *Arnkerrth* as an exceedingly clever, physically and mentally tough Old Lizard Woman.

Metonymy is the key trope linking the visual representation of *Arnkerrth* to the greatly expanded oral version of this Dreaming narrative.[8] This is the case with all 'classical' Centralian and Western Desert art (see Cataldi 1998 and Nicholls 1998, for more on this). The iconography Petyarre employs to portray *Arnkerrth*'s expeditions can be understood as a metonymic device or 'visual language' in which a *part* is used to represent an *entire* narrative. In this instance, *Arnkerrth*'s diminutive, semi-circular patterns of tracks stand for the entire epic pilgrimage undertaken by the small creature, acting as a metaphor for, and mirroring the journey of, life itself.

The unsolicited coming of the white interlopers to Petyarre's family's country has invited new possibilities for contemporary, even post-colonial, readings of the *Arnkerrth* Dreaming narrative. This cataclysmic event brings a new dimension to this epic saga. *Arnkerrth*'s ability to deal with adversity, the now exponentially increased danger and complications that arise as she attempts to negotiate her way through her own country, and her dealings with those who cross her path, friendly or otherwise, all represent new versions of old challenges. But, as a result of her early period of learning the complex art and science of survival, *Arnkerrth* is unfailingly prepared. One lesson to be derived from the *Arnkerrth* Dreaming narrative is that uncertainty is certain, unpredictability is actually quite foreseeable, and therefore one should always have one's strategies at the ready.

Implicit in this however, is a challenge offered to viewers and collectors of Petyarre's work: endeavouring to come to terms with the range of meanings of *Arnkerrth* and the narrative in which she is framed.

Is Kathleen Petyarre a Great Artist? (Or, Landscape, Truth and Beauty)

To answer this question, one first must ask by whose socio-cultural standards are we to judge? Anmatyerr artists do not differentiate between Dreamings or paintings in terms of their spiritual or purely visual significance, so the level of technical competence in the creation and re-creation of individual works is never really an issue. For this reason, the 'western' practice of singling out artists for special praise is a mystery to those Anmatyerr whose works remain unconsecrated by the art market, and therefore less wanted or unwanted. But, because Kathleen has a thorough and grounded knowledge of the Mountain Devil Dreaming, there is no question that she is highly respected as an artist by her fellow Anmatyerr.

Yet the Anmatyerr have been recently and rudely propelled into a world dominated by the socio-economic norms of late capitalism, and their paintings are no longer judged simply by their *use* value, but to a much greater extent than previously by their *exchange* value. Like other art work in an increasingly global market, Anmatyerr art, including that of Kathleen Petyarre, has now been thrust into the world of circulating and trading commodities. If the work of an Indigenous artist does not garner the art world's respect, including that of the dealers, collectors and critics, it will not acquire value through the market.

The alienation of the work from its conditions of production and its producer is something of a puzzle to many Centralian and Western Desert people. Nevertheless they are aware of the existence of a different set of criteria brought to bear in judging the worth of a painting. Kathleen has worked hard at determining, understanding and negotiating those criteria and shows mastery over them.

Petyarre is highly disciplined as an artist. Each of her compositions is very carefully organised, relying on a grid pattern that she maps out in detail before commencing each work. Many hours are spent in canvas preparation, carefully applying the gesso in a way that allows layer upon layer of different coloured paints to become absorbed into the linen. It is this absorption of colours and layers into the canvas that gives Petyarre's work its very 'fine', or even 'refined' appearance – a factor which differentiates it from a great deal of contemporary Indigenous art. Because the colour of the paint becomes diluted as successive layers are applied and soak into the canvas, this heightens the illusion of three-dimensionality. It sometimes gives the impression that the earth has been sliced open, so that we feel that we are looking from above at the earth's surface dissected. Petyarre's restrained palette, mostly restricted to 'earth' colours, compounds this impression.

Her dotting is part of each work's texture – the dots don't just 'sit' lumpily atop the canvas. This is in contrast with a good deal of contemporary Indigenous painting, which is seemingly executed with hasty passion, and has become decreasingly attractive to, and less valorised by, the market in recent years.

Underneath the screen of very fine dotting Kathleen's Dreaming exists as a barely tangible, shadowy palimpsest, overlaid by the luminous surface colours which gradually change tone. Nodes of colour shift seamlessly through the work. The layers upon layers on the scarcely discernible grid create a strong sense of abstraction, an alchemical atmosphere. *Arnkerrth*, the journey woman, the Dreaming Ancestor, is glimpsed sometimes as a trick of the surface, sometimes as a tantalising subterranean presence sensed or felt by the viewer rather than actually seen. *Arnkerrth*'s tracks, as she makes her way through the harsh desert conditions, become a whirling vortex. The layering effect and the illusion of spiralling movement that come from Kathleen's sheer technical brilliance are almost certainly by-products of her earlier familiarity with body painting, learned during her youth and early adulthood, and later with the technically demanding methods of batik.

The layering effect signifies the ability of *Arnkerrth* to camouflage herself no matter how challenging the terrain. By metaphoric extension this suggests that what takes place beneath the earth's crust is equally, if not more, significant than that which can be seen by the naked eye. *Arnkerrth* has the ability to alternately reveal and disguise herself by going in and out of the earth's surface, all the while bearing her lode of ground red ochre in preparation for the forthcoming ceremony. Her passage through climatic extremes is suggested by the muted array of oscillating, variegated colours that Petyarre so skilfully applies to her canvasses.

These groupings of tiny colourful specks or dots Petyarre applies using the sharp end of satay sticks, which she purchases in commercial quantities during her travels to Indonesia (she goes through thousands of sticks in any working year). The visual effect of this controlled explosion of very fine dots, which give Petyarre's works their exquisitely stippled 'fine art' look, means that a non-Anmatyerr viewer does not have to be aware of *Arnkerrth*'s presence in Petyarre's work to appreciate it. Petyarre's uncanny ability to imply layers of meaning invites many possible readings of her work, thereby both incorporating and transcending exclusively Anmatyerr interpretations, and simultaneously fulfilling spiritually hungry non-Indigenous audiences who are seeking depth. Art critics have unselfconsciously discussed Petyarre's work in terms of Kant's theory of the sublime, and compared it with New York-based Ross Bleckner's hypnotic conceptual studies of the molecular world of DNA and cell structure.

Yet ultimately control is exercised over the work by its underlying Dreaming and the power of Petyarre's work emanates from this truth. Kathleen Petyarre manages to keep the substratum of sacred meaning intact, evoking rather than disclosing her Dreaming. As Aboriginal cultures tend towards being cultures of concealment rather than cultures of revelation this is a move at once pragmatic, strategic and poetic.

Kathleen Petyarre is among that handful of Indigenous Australian artists whose work has contributed to opening up what had become pigeonholed as 'Indigenous Australian art' to a broader set of possible meanings. Her work permits a kind of multiple vision: not only is it deeply meaningful to other Indigenous groups as religious art of the Dreaming but it may be also read as abstract, expressionist, impressionist, minimalist or even post-modern, and most certainly as post-ethnographic.

It is perhaps ironic, given the facts of Kathleen's life, that her works seem equally at home in New York, Paris, or Sydney as they do at her own 'place', Atnangker. Like the late Emily Kngwarreye, Kathleen Petyarre draws upon the Indigenous to create the international.

Taking a different kind of 'horizonal' perspective than she has in the past, in recent years Kathleen has been attempting to create what she describes as a 'new style', evoking the sense of 'travelling in a light plane, like it's moving, travelling, looking down'. Yet Kathleen is adamant that although she's not afraid to innovate:

It's still body painting, still ceremony, even looking from the sky [it is] still dancing, still ceremony, my new style is still dancing ceremony.

Ultimately, Kathleen's paintings meet the artistic and cultural criteria of both the Eastern Anmatyerr and the dominant culture. While her methods may have changed in the course of the sometimes tempestuous changes and challenges she has experienced in her lifetime, Petyarre remains true to the spiritual subject matter of her paintings, loyal to her Dreaming Ancestor, and therefore to herself.

Petyarre also succeeds *par excellence* in performing the double dance. This may well guarantee her a kind of immortality. Even those who have little or no understanding of Petyarre's subject matter can appreciate the grandeur and power of her work.

Acknowledgements

I am extremely indebted to the following people, all of whom have helped immeasurably in the making of this book: first and foremost, Kweyetwemp (Kathleen) Petyarre, who generously gave many hours of her time for the interviews which are the foundation on which my essay rests, and from which excerpts are quoted throughout the text; her sister Violet Petyarre who was present during many of the interviews and also offered valuable comments on the sisters' shared past and present; David Cossey and particularly Penelope Hoile, of Gallerie Australis, Adelaide; Jenny Green, a linguist working on the Anmatyerr language at the Institute for Aboriginal Development in Alice Springs, whose generous help with Anmatyerr language and orthography has been invaluable, as has her willingness to share her knowledge about the history of the art movement at Utopia; Rodney Gooch, former art co-ordinator at Utopia, for sharing some of his perspectives on the past; Nick Richardson, whose assistance in a variety of ways, particularly with identifying maps of Anmatyerr country, has been marvellous; Maggie Fletcher, of Flinders University Art Museum, for her computer skills and assistance with the diagram of Kathleen's painting; Frank and Anne

Brennan, for sharing with me some of their past experiences from the time that they were living at Utopia; Professor Diane Bell for permission to reproduce photographs that were taken during the Utopia Land Claim; Christopher Hodges for permission to reproduce a photograph; and Professor Michael Chesterman of the University of New South Wales, Sydney, for legal advice. In addition, I would like to thank the following people for reading earlier drafts of this manuscript, and for their valuable comments: first and foremost, Jenny Green; as well as Ian North, Sue Williams, Dione McDonald, Sally Tingle, Maggie Fletcher, Sandra Maynard and Helen Bonnet.

Notes

1 (Atneltyey 1988, Iylenty 1998); (Jenny Green, in Ryan, ed., 1998:44)

2 See Richardson 2001 for a full account of the history of western schooling at Utopia from 1969.

3 Hilda 'Cookie' Pwerl, in conversation with Jenny Green, February 2001, recalls a school trip to Wollongong and elsewhere taking place later than this.

4 Sic – note changes in Anmatyerr orthography over the years.

5 See for example the work of linguists such as Liberman 1981; 1982; 1985; Kaldor and Malcolm, 1991; Eades 1991; 1992; 1994; 1995; Nicholls 1998.

6 Nicholls, Christine, 2000, 'Kathleen Petyarre', transcribed artist's statement and catalogue essay, in Brenda L. Croft (Editor and Curator), *Beyond The Pale, Contemporary Indigenous Art*, 2000 Adelaide Biennial of Australian Art, Art Gallery of South Australia, Adelaide, Australia, pp 65–69.

7 Cf. Walter Pater: '*all art constantly aspires toward the condition of music*' (his italics), in 'The School of Giorgione', first pub. 1877, in *Walter Pater, The Renaissance: Studies in Art and Poetry* (1888), (New York: Mentor Books, 1959), 95.

8 Kathleen Petyarre related the *Arnkerrth* Dreaming narrative to me in September 2000 in the presence of her sister Violet Petyarre, while we were all staying in Bali.

GALLERY

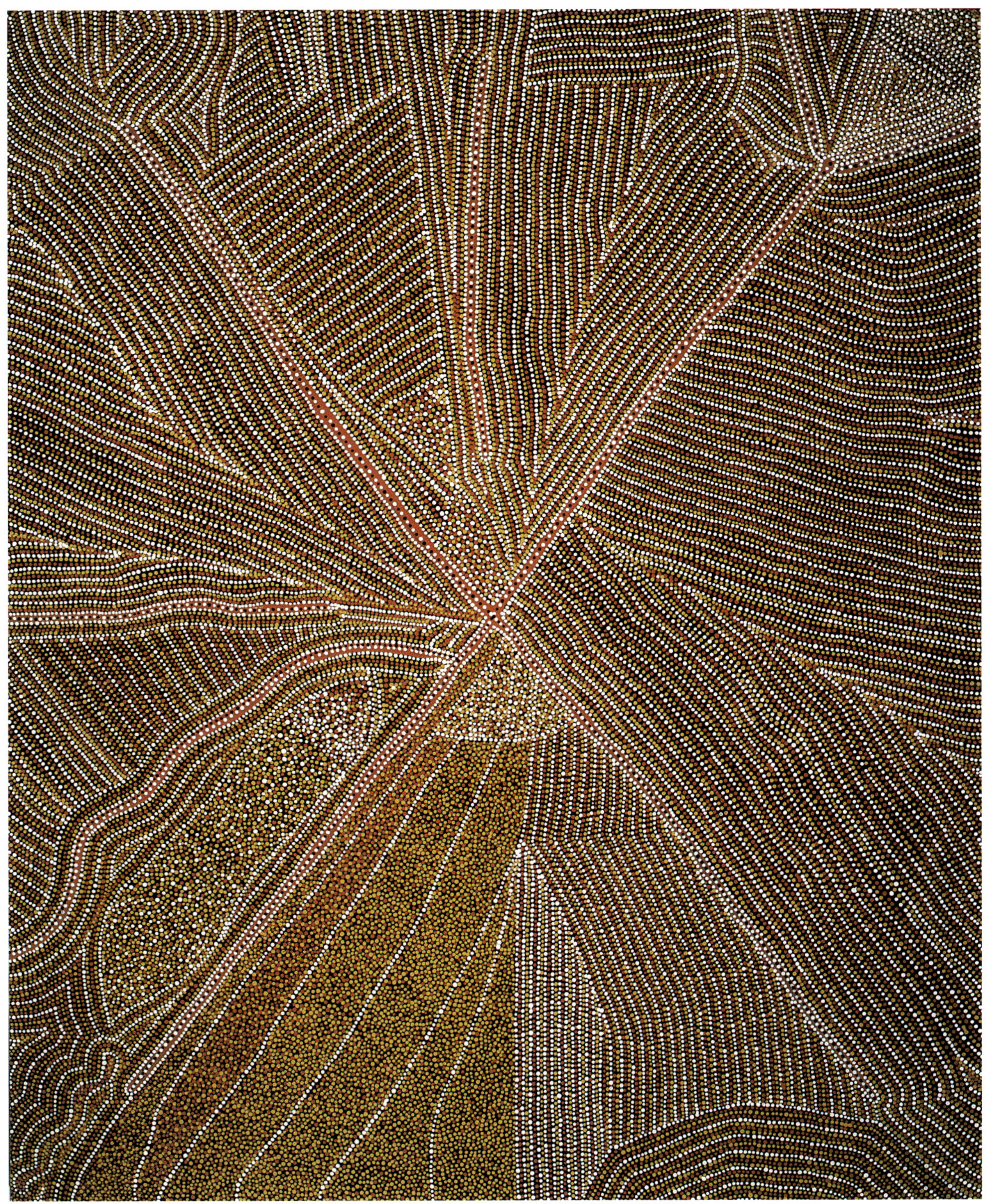

Mountain Devil Lizard Dreaming 1991 Synthetic polymer paint on Belgian linen 152 x 122 cm (5' x 4') Private collection, Switzerland

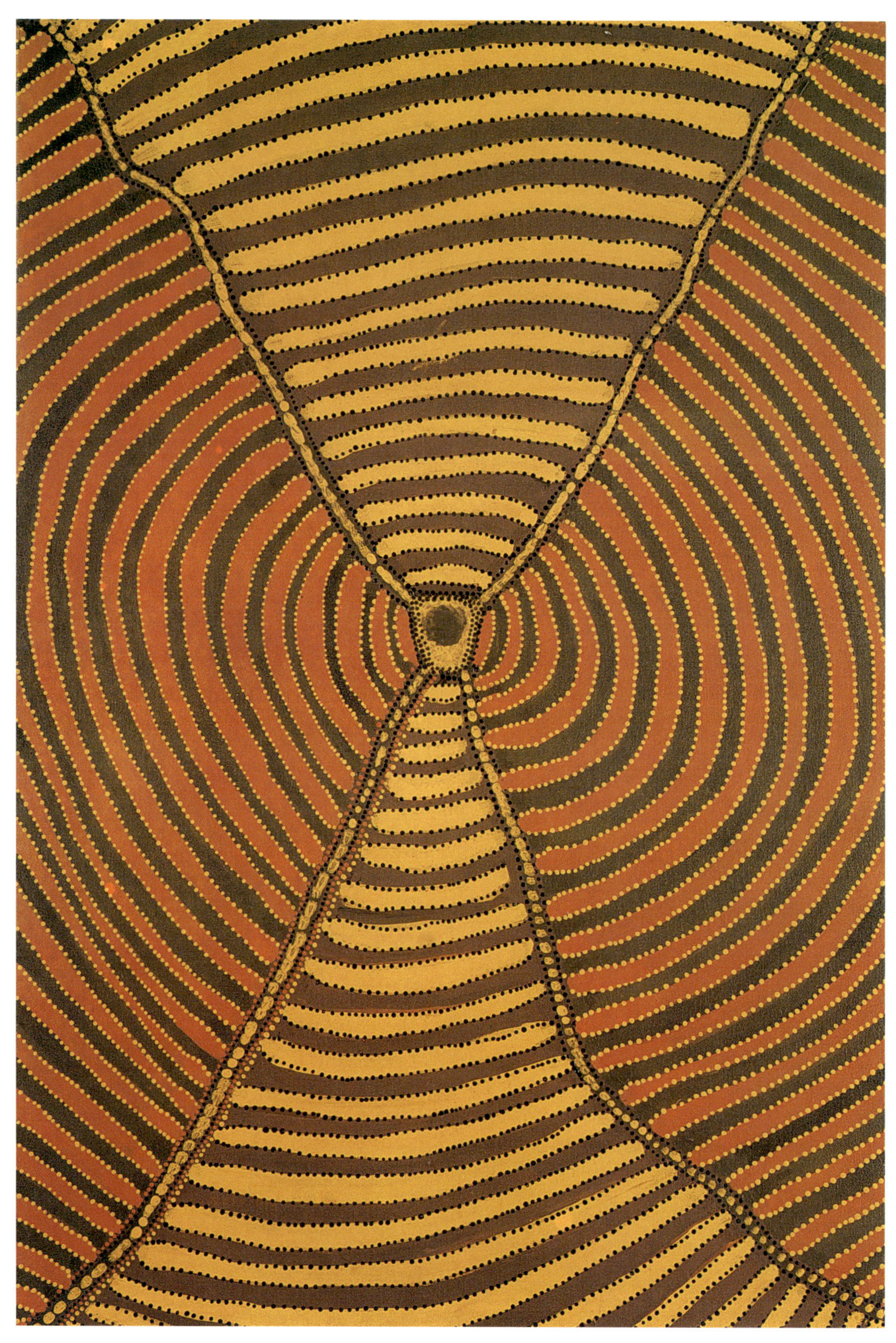

Emu Dreaming 1992 Synthetic polymer paint on Belgian linen 91 x 61 cm (3' x 2') Private collection, Adelaide, Australia

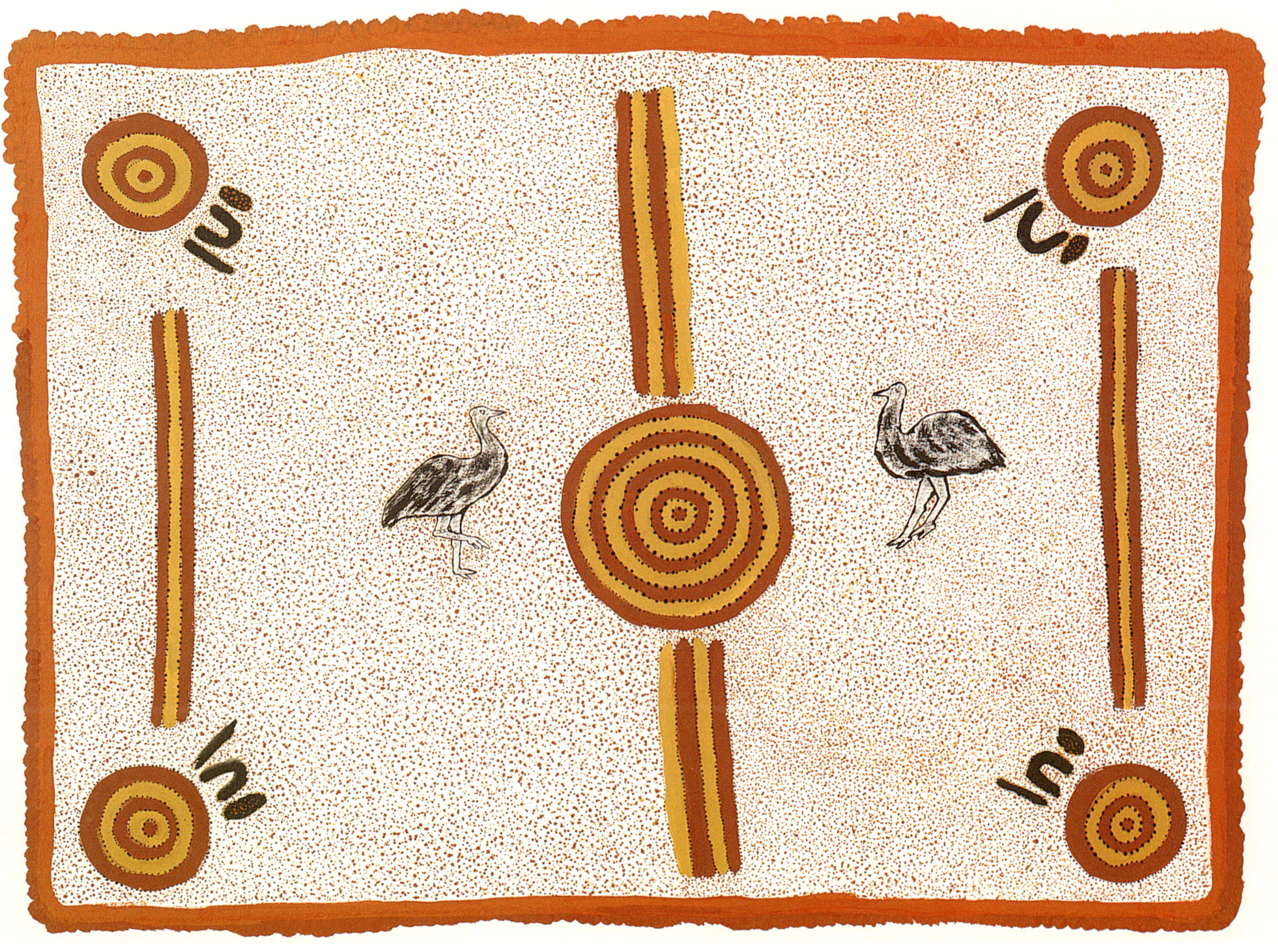

Emu Dreaming c.1993 Synthetic polymer paint on Arches Paper 57.5 x 76.5 cm (1'10½" x 2'6") Private collection, courtesy of Gallerie Australis, Adelaide, Australia

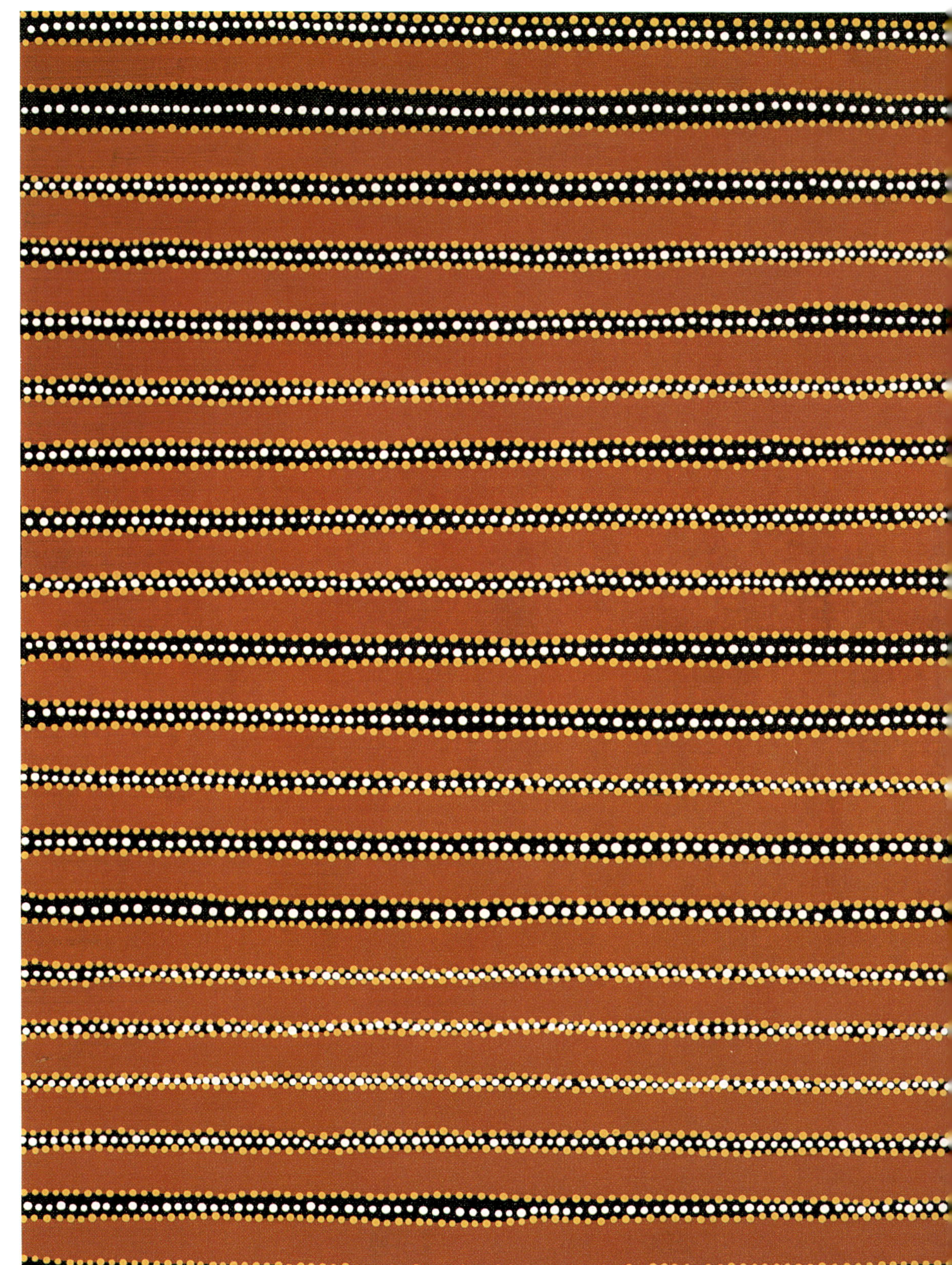

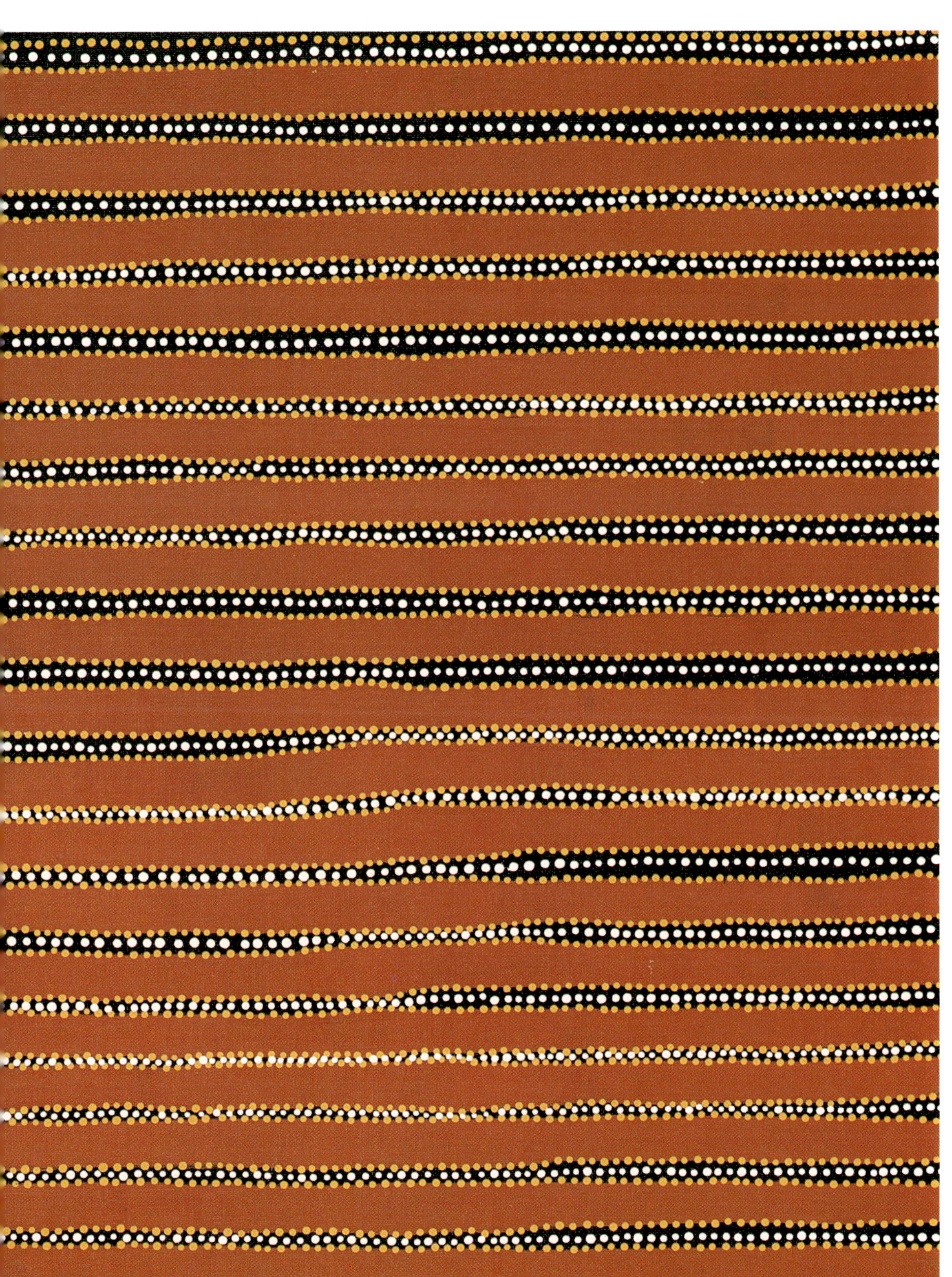

Emu Dreaming 1994

Synthetic polymer paint on canvas board 60.5 x 76 cm (2' x 2'6)

Private collection, courtesy of Gallerie Australis, Adelaide, Australia

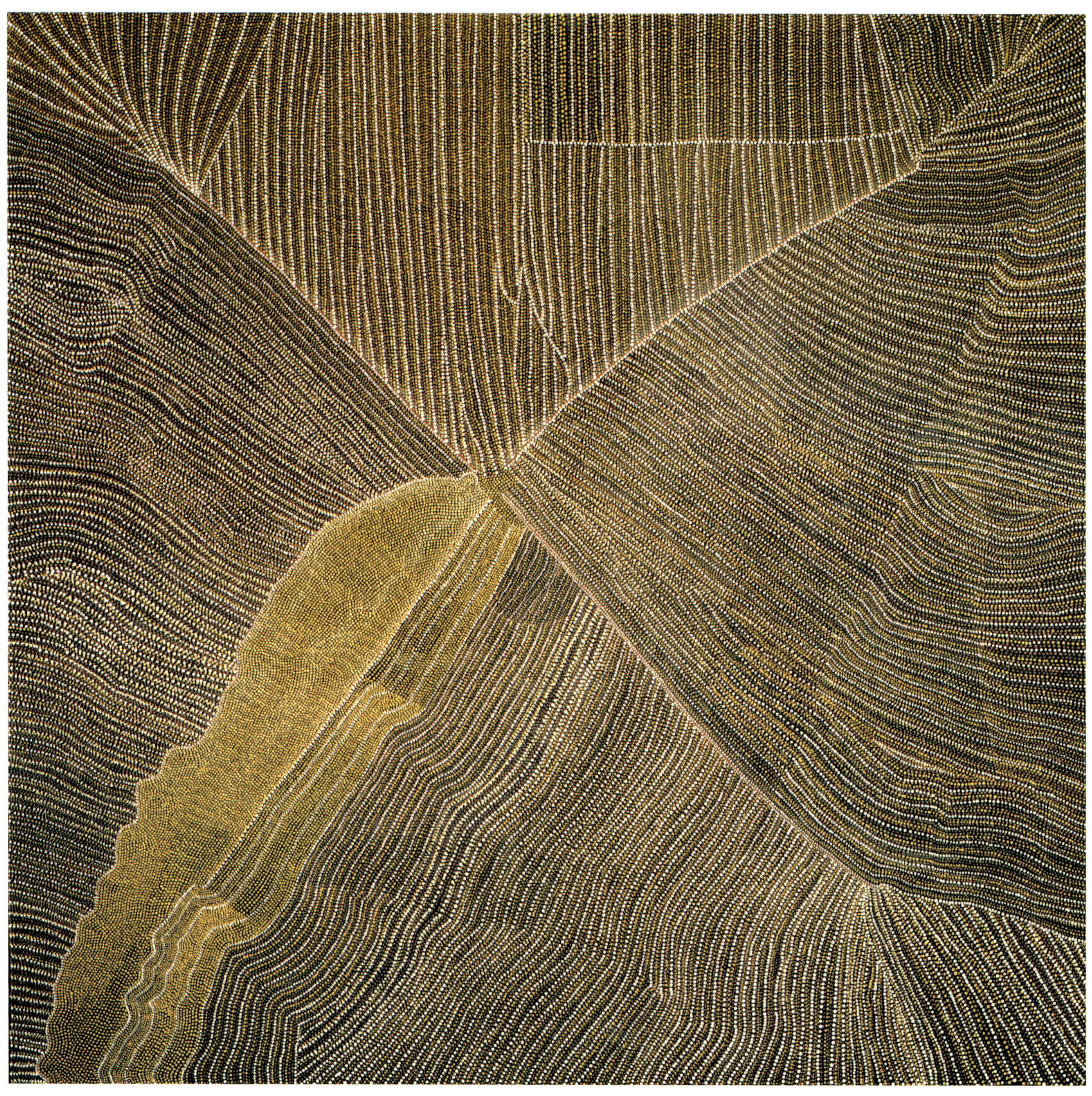

Mountain Devil Lizard Dreaming 1995 Synthetic polymer paint on Belgian linen 152 x 152 cm (5' x 5') Private collection, Switzerland

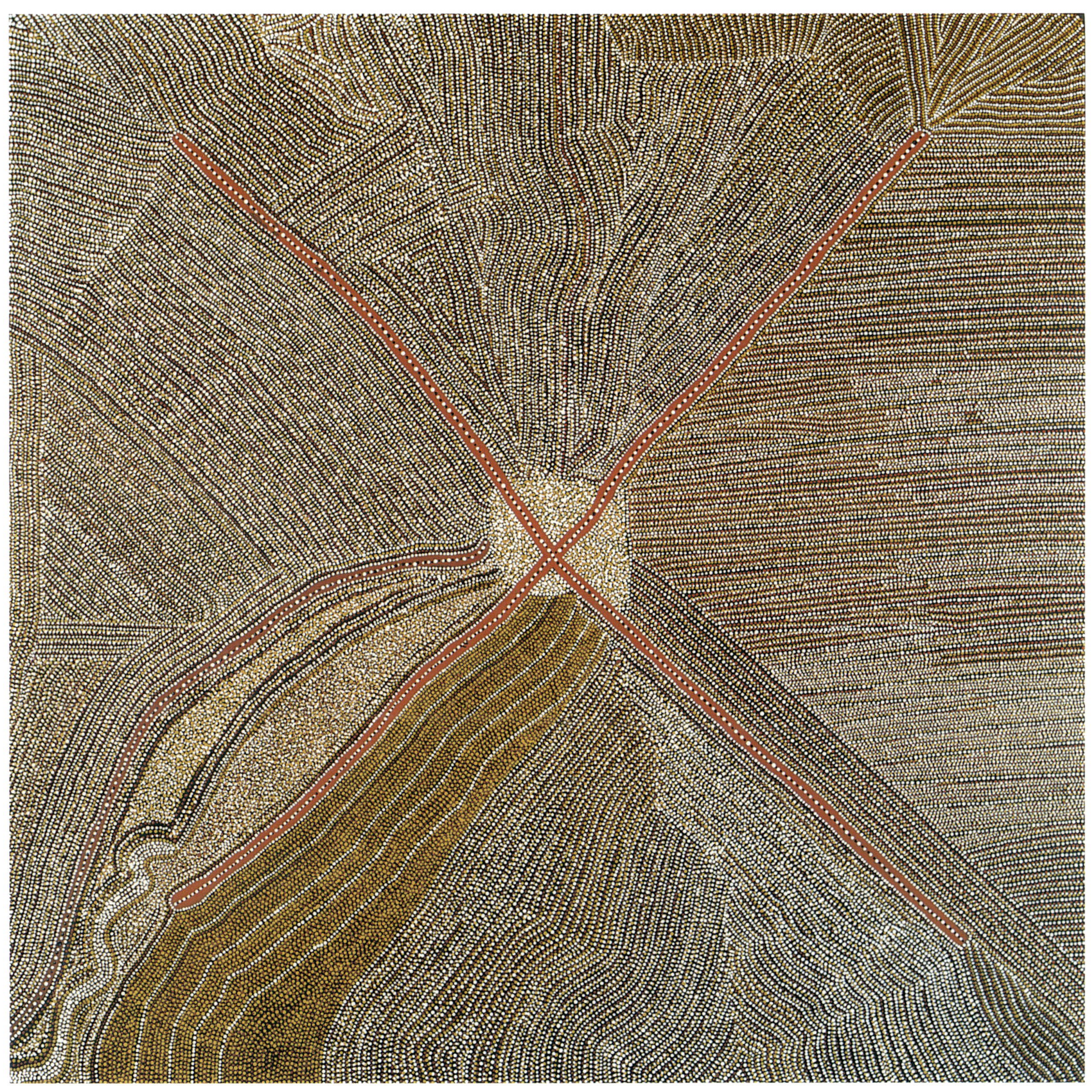

Mountain Devil Lizard Dreaming 1995 Synthetic polymer paint on Belgian linen 152 x 152 cm (5' x 5') Private collection, Sydney, Australia

Thorny Devil Lizard Dreaming (Hailstorm) 1995 Synthetic polymer paint on Belgian linen 122 x 183 cm (4' x 6') Private collection, Melbourne, Australia

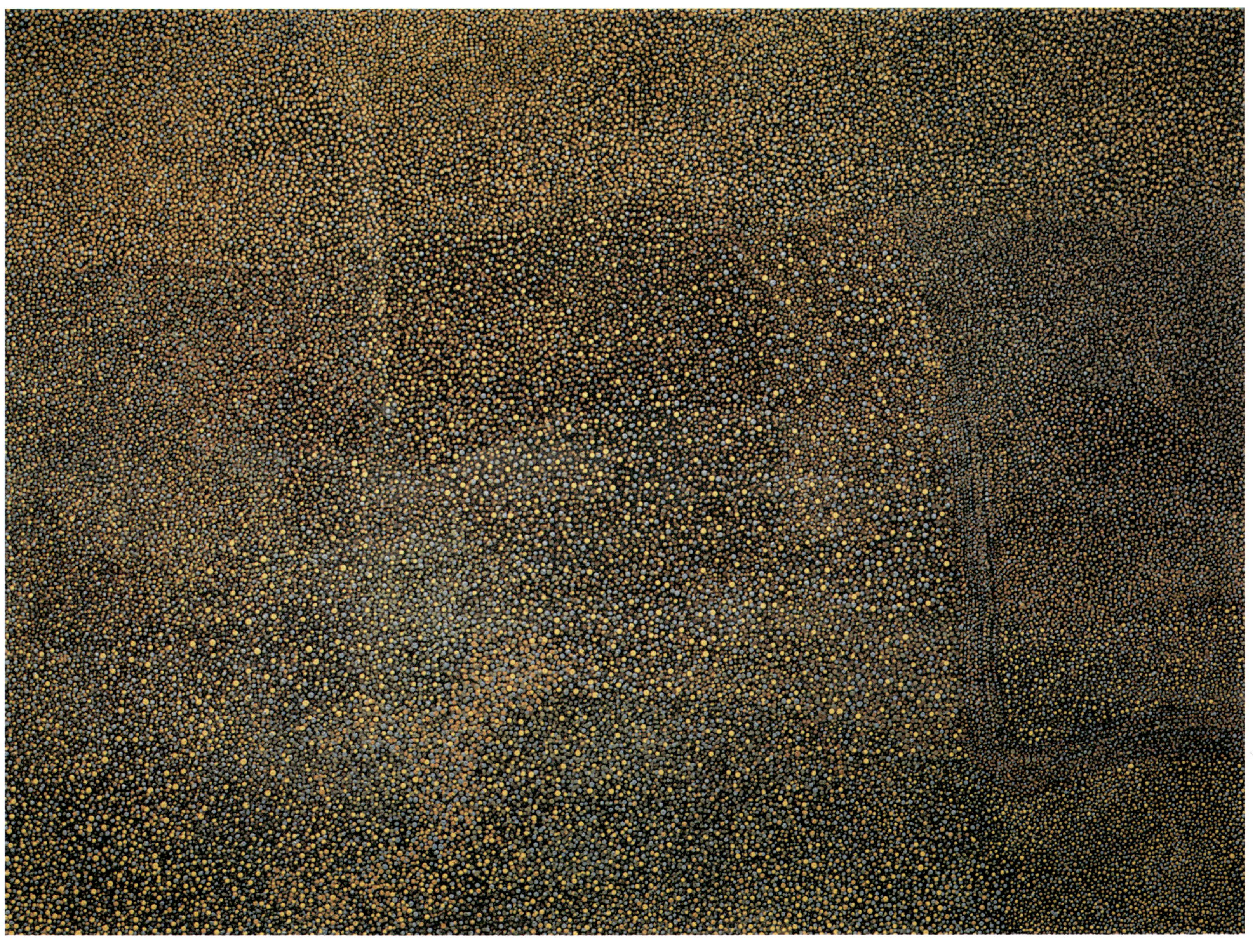

Thorny Devil Lizard Dreaming 1995 Synthetic polymer paint on Belgian linen 91 x 122 cm (3' x 4') The Kelton Foundation, California, United States of America

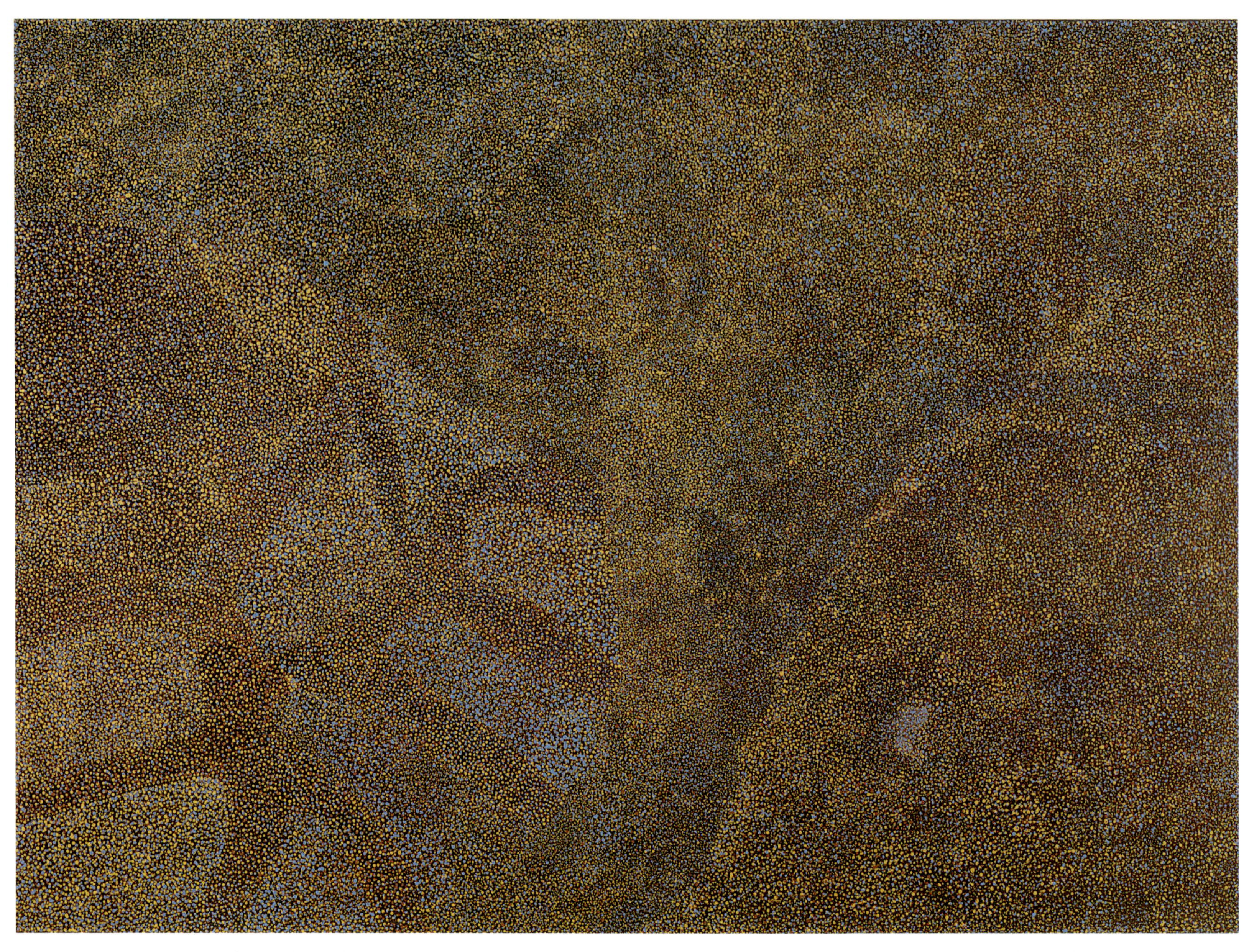

Thorny Devil Lizard Dreaming (Watercourses & Rockholes) 1996 Synthetic polymer paint on Belgian linen 91.5 x 122 cm (3' x 4') Private collection, Melbourne, Australia

Thorny Devil Lizard Dreaming (Autumn) 1996 Synthetic polymer paint on Belgian linen 122 x 183 cm (4' x 6') Private collection, Melbourne, Australia

Dreaming Country of the Thorny Devil Lizard (After Sandstorm) 1996

Synthetic polymer paint on Belgian linen 122 x 183 cm (4' x 6') Thomas Vroom Collection, The Netherlands. Awarded Joint Second Prize in the Australian Heritage Commission's Third National Aboriginal & Torres Strait Islander Heritage Art Award – The Art of the Place in Canberra on 2 April 1996

Dreaming Country of the Thorny Devil Lizard 1996 Synthetic polymer paint on Belgian linen 152.5 x 152.5 cm (5' x 5') Thomas Vroom Collection, The Netherlands

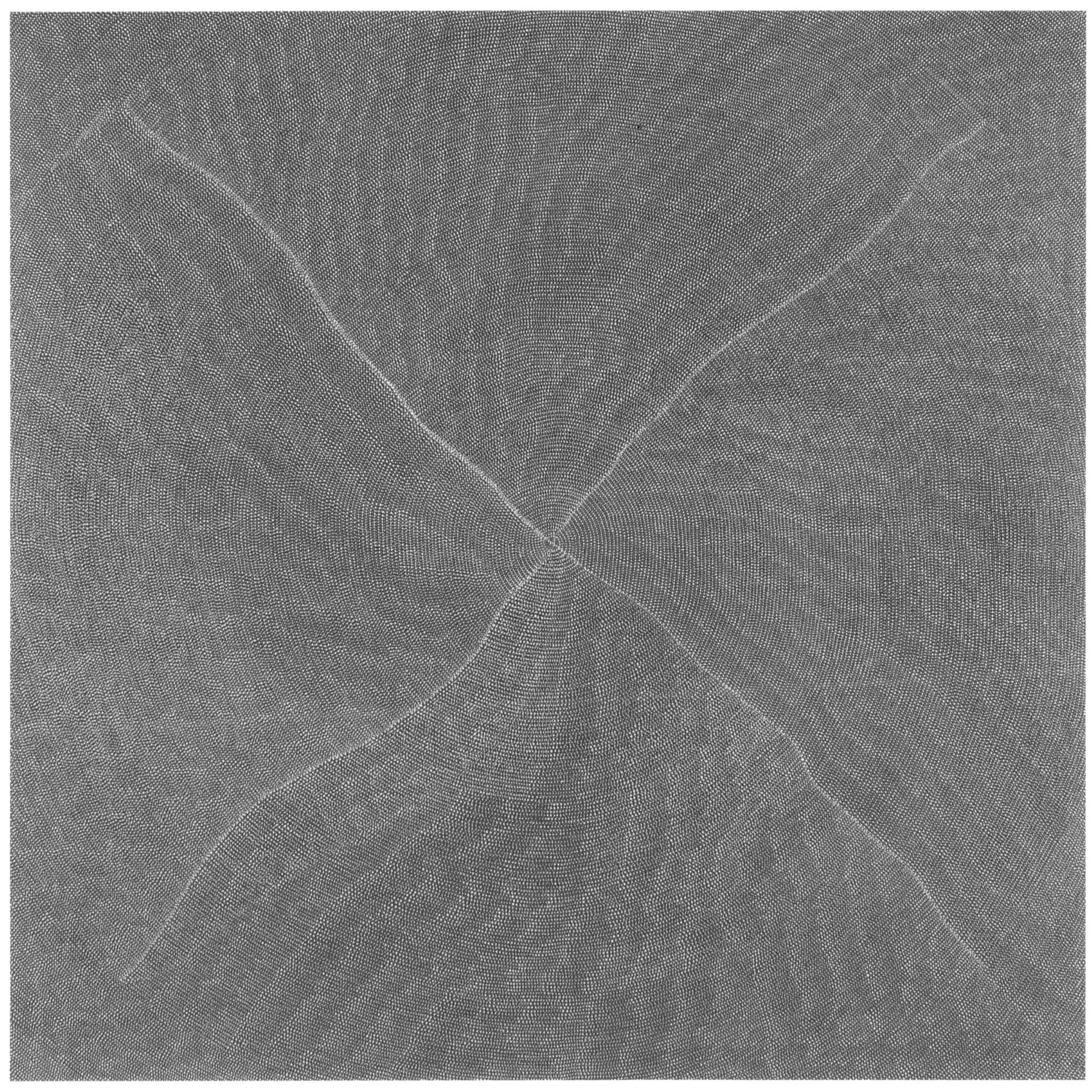

Storm in Atnangkere Country II 1996 Synthetic polymer paint on Belgian linen 182.5 x 182. 5 cm (6' x 6') Telstra Collection, Museum and Art Gallery of the Northern Territory, Darwin, Australia, purchased 1996. Winner of the 13th National Aboriginal & Torres Strait Islander Art Award

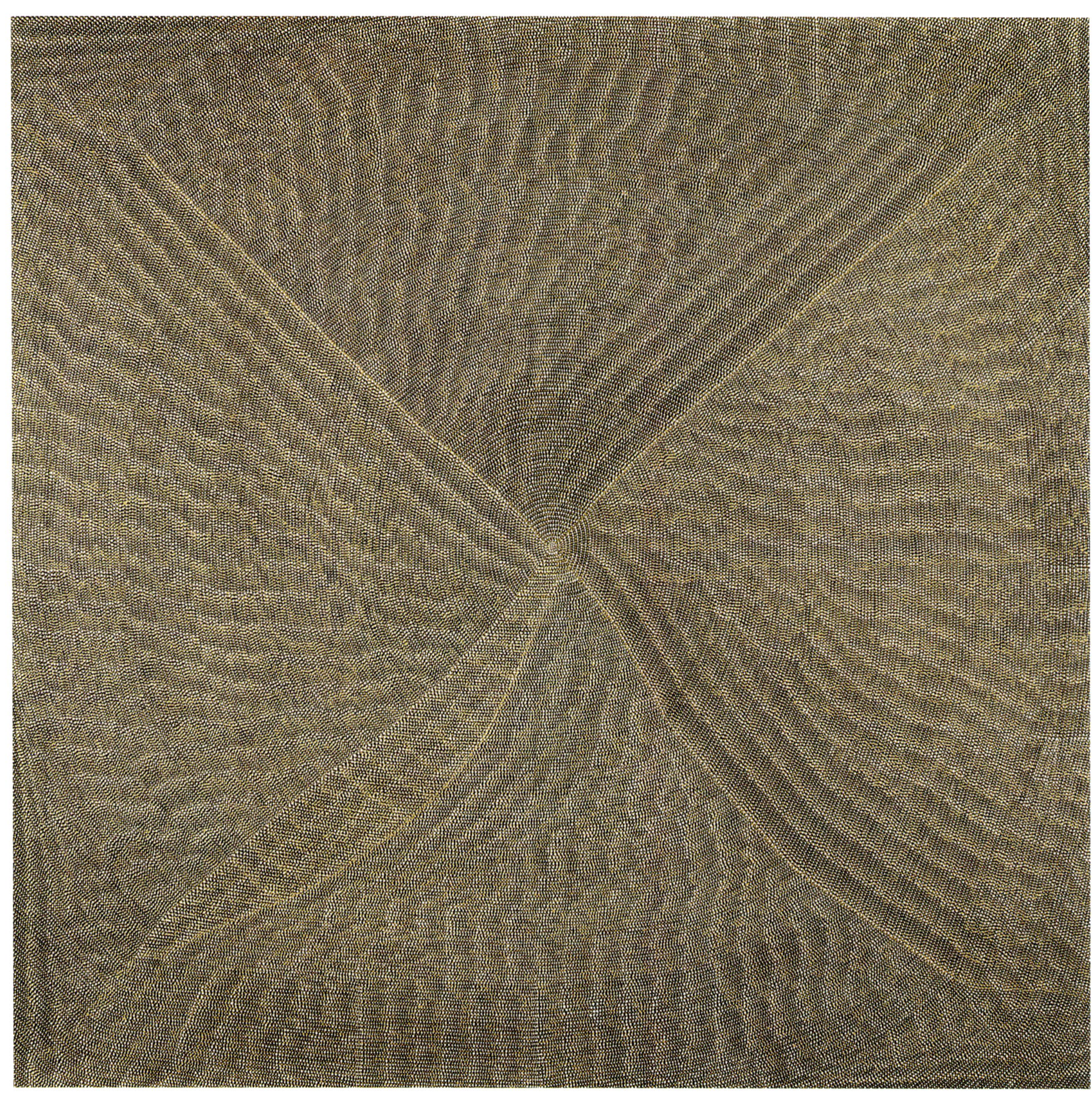

Mountain Devil Lizard Dreaming (With Winter Sandstorm) 1996 Synthetic polymer paint on Belgian linen 183 x 183 cm (6' x 6') Art Gallery of South Australia, Adelaide, Australia, Aileen Thompson Bequest Fund through the Art Gallery of South Australia

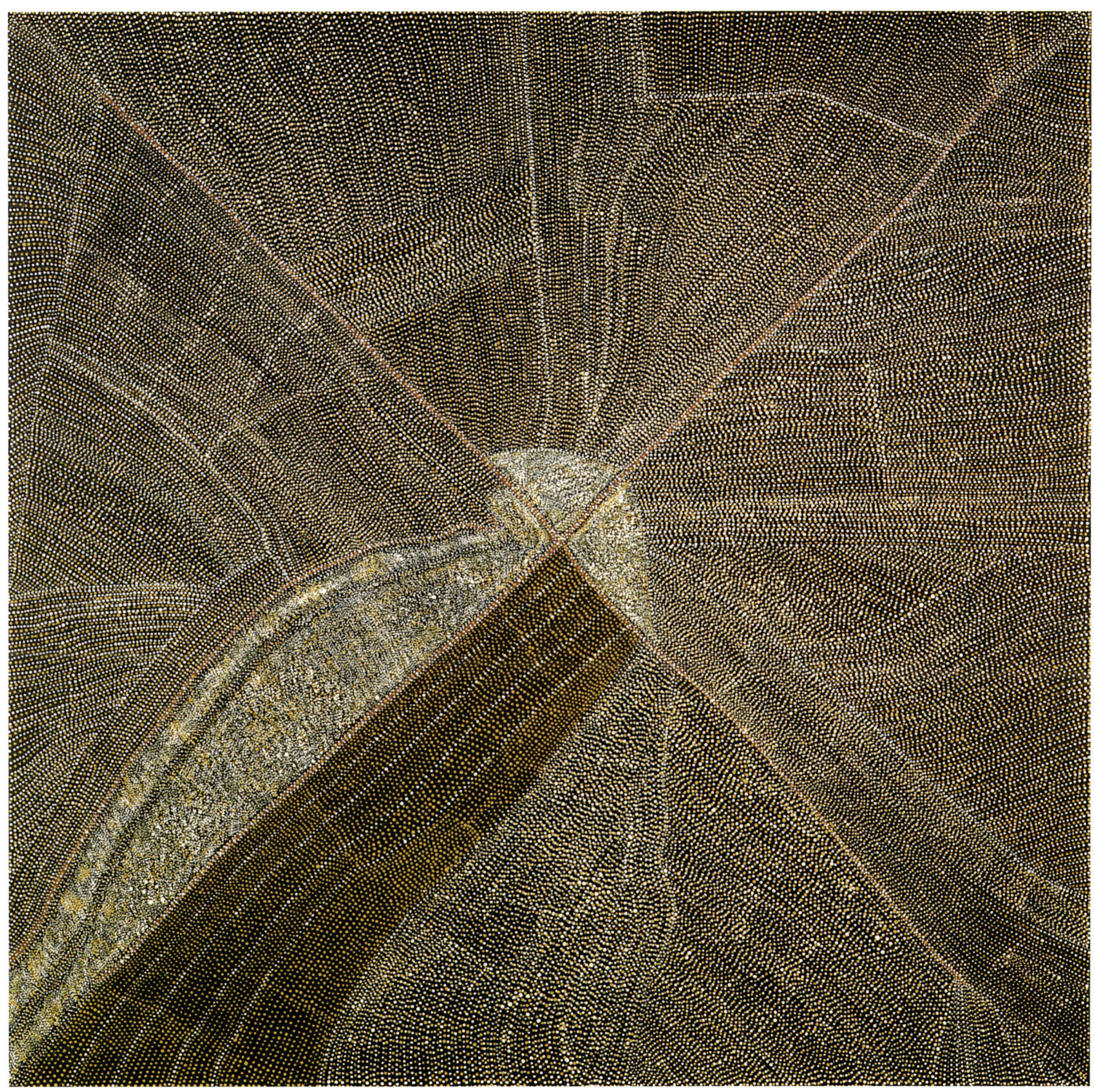

Mountain Devil Lizard Dreaming 1997 Synthetic polymer paint on Belgian linen 122 x 122 cm (4' x 4') Thomas Vroom Collection, The Netherlands

My Country – Bush Seeds 1997 Synthetic polymer paint on Belgian linen 244 x 243 cm (8' x 7'11¾") Kerry Stokes Collection, Perth, Australia. Commissioned for the John McCaughey Memorial Art Award 1997/1998 by the National Gallery of Victoria, Melbourne, Australia

(Right) *My Country – Bush Seeds 1997 (Detail)*

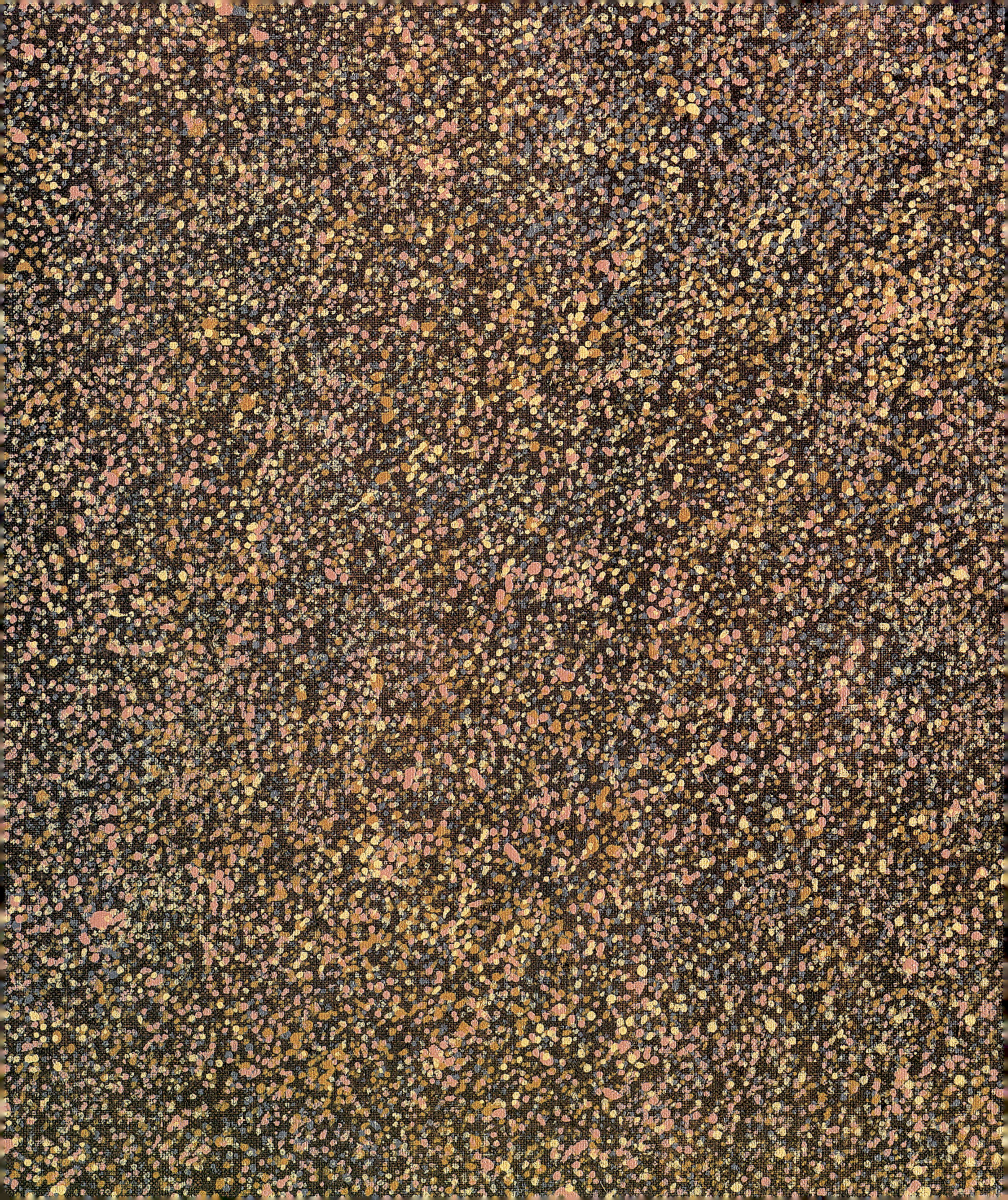

Thorny Devil Lizard Dreaming (Watercourses & Rockholes)
1997

Synthetic polymer paint on Belgian linen 122 x 183 cm (4' x 6')
University of South Australia Art Collection, Adelaide, Australia

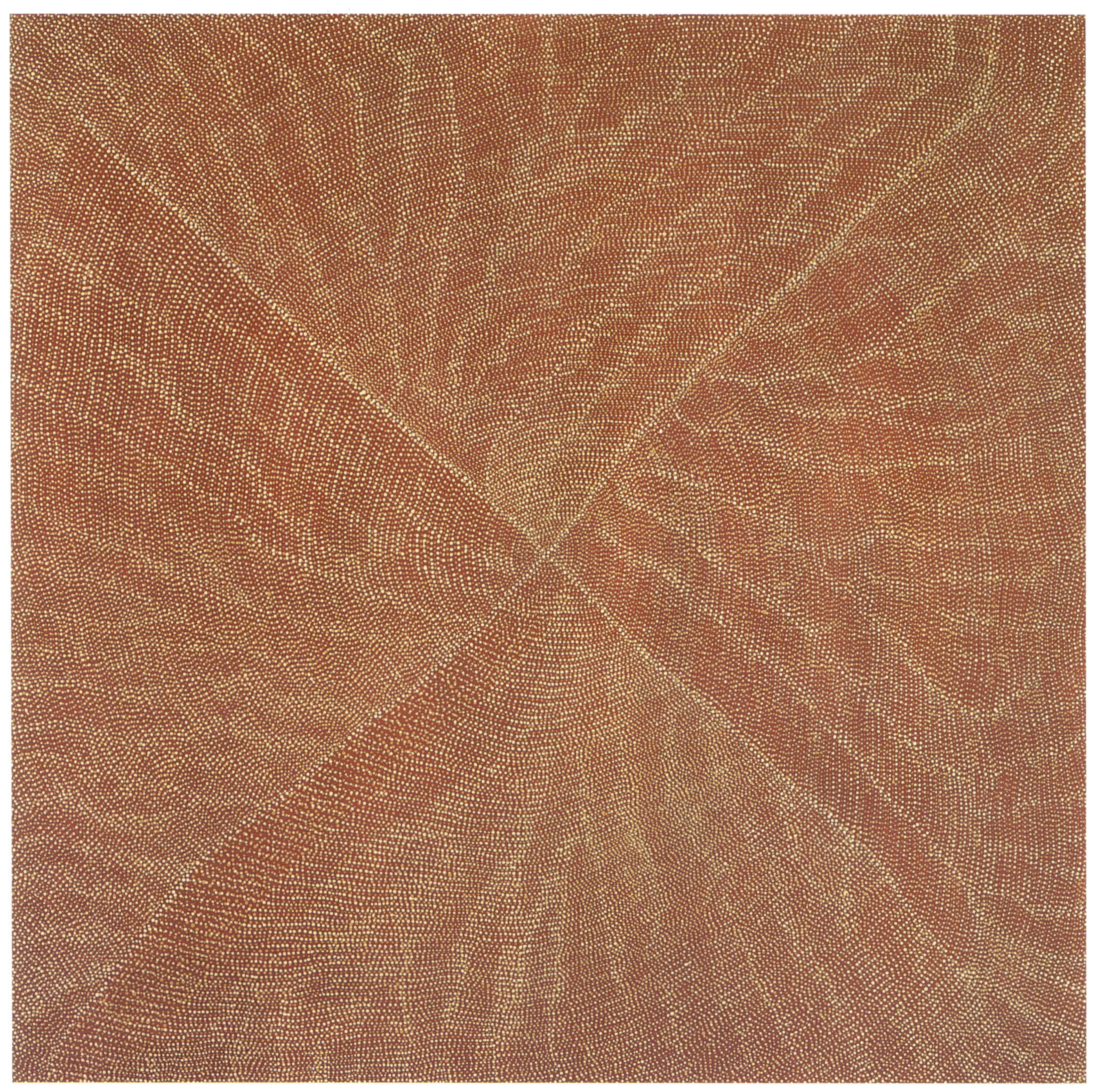

Mountain Devil Lizard Dreaming (After Sandstorm) 1998 Synthetic polymer paint on Belgian linen 122 x 122 cm (4' x 4') Private collection, Melbourne, Australia

My Country – Bush Seeds 1998 Synthetic polymer paint on Belgian linen 244 x 244 cm (8' x 8') Art Gallery of South Australia, Adelaide, Australia, Santos Fund for Aboriginal Art 1999

Thorny Devil Lizard Dreaming (Watercourses & Rockholes) 1997 Synthetic polymer paint on Belgian linen 122 x 183 cm (4' x 6') Thomas Vroom Collection, The Netherlands

My Country - Bush Seeds 1998 Synthetic polymer paint on Belgian linen 183 x 244 cm (6' x 8') Private collection, courtesy of Gallerie Australis, Adelaide, Australia

My Country – Bush Seeds (Hailstorm) 1998 Synthetic polymer paint on Belgian linen 122 x 152.5 cm (4' x 5') Private collection, Sydney, Australia

My Country – Bush Seeds (Hailstorm) 2001 Synthetic polymer paint on Belgian linen 183 x 183 cm (6' x 6') The James and Jacqui Erskine Collection, Sydney, Australia

My Country – Bush Seeds 1998 Synthetic polymer paint on Belgian linen 152 x 152 cm (5' x 5') Levi-Kaplan Collection, Seattle, United States of America

My Country – Bush Seeds (Sandstorm) 1999 Synthetic polymer paint on Belgian linen 183 x 183 cm (6' x 6') Private collection, courtesy of Gallerie Australis, Adelaide, Australia

Thorny Devil Lizard Dreaming (Watercourses & Rockholes) 2001

Synthetic polymer paint on Belgian linen 122 x 183 cm (4'x 6')

Levi-Kaplan collection, Seattle, United States of America

Thorny Devil Lizard Dreaming (Watercourses & Rockholes) 1999 Synthetic polymer paint on Belgian linen 122 x 183 cm (4' x 6') Thomas Vroom Collection, The Netherlands

(Right) *Thorny Devil Lizard Dreaming (Watercourses & Rockholes) 1999 (Detail)*

Mountain Devil Lizard Dreaming – Sandhill Country (Sandstorm) 1999 Synthetic polymer paint on Belgian linen 122 x 122 cm (4' x 4') Levi-Kaplan Collection, Seattle, United States of America

Mountain Devil Lizard Dreaming - Sandhill Country (Sandstorm) 1999 Synthetic polymer paint on Belgian linen 183 x 183 cm (6' x 6') Private collection, courtesy of Coo-ee Aboriginal Art, Sydney, Australia

Mountain Devil Lizard Dreaming – Sandhill Country 1999 Synthetic polymer paint on Belgian linen 183 x 183 cm (6' x 6') Private collection, courtesy of Coo-ee Aboriginal Art, Sydney, Australia

Mountain Devil Lizard Dreaming – Sandhill Country (After Hailstorm) 1999 Synthetic polymer paint on Belgian linen 183 x 183 cm (6' x 6')

Private collection, courtesy of Gallerie Australis, Adelaide, Australia

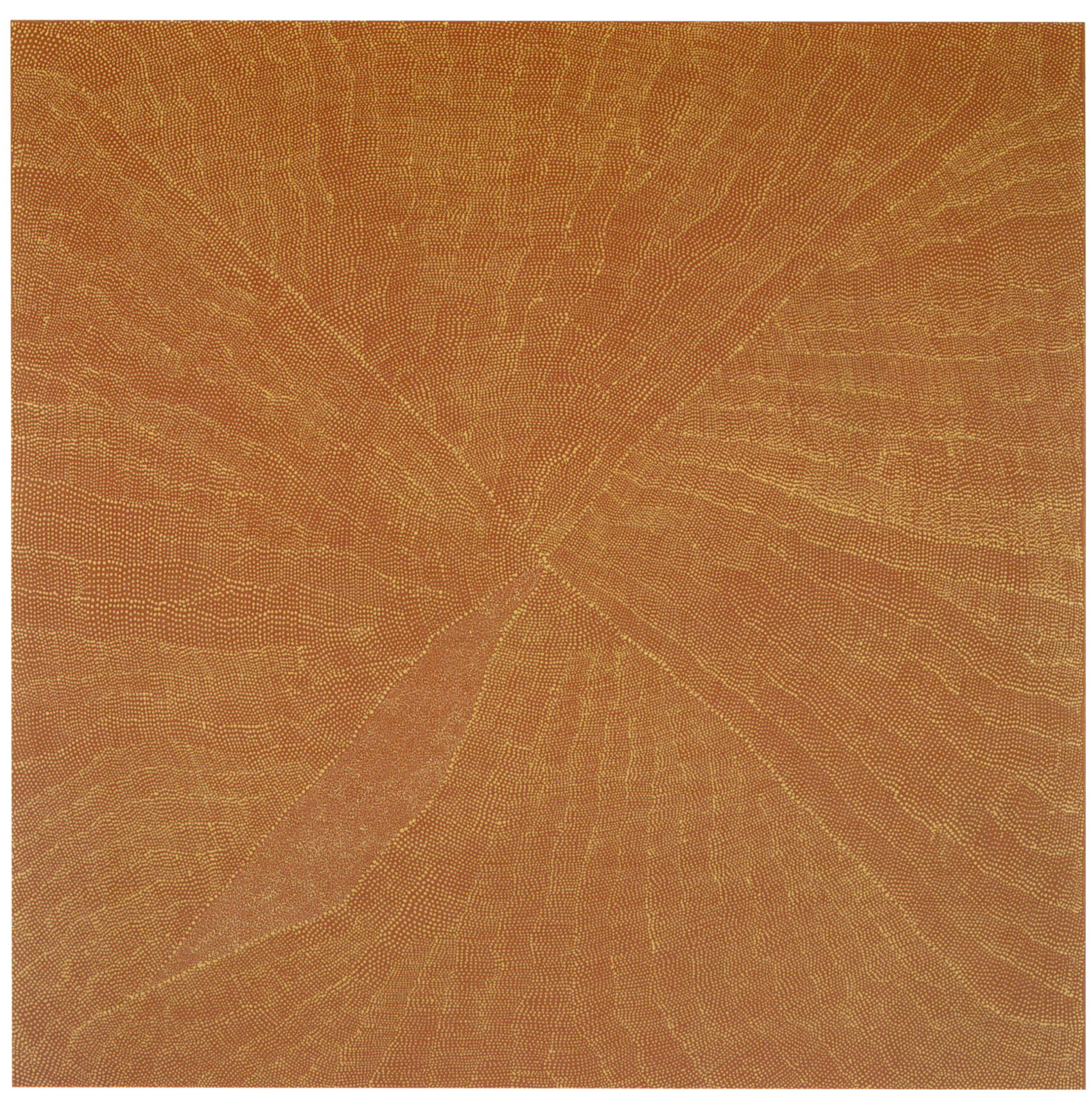

Mountain Devil Lizard Dreaming (Sandstorm) 2000 Synthetic polymer paint on Belgian linen 122 x 122 cm (4' x 4') Private collection, Adelaide, Australia

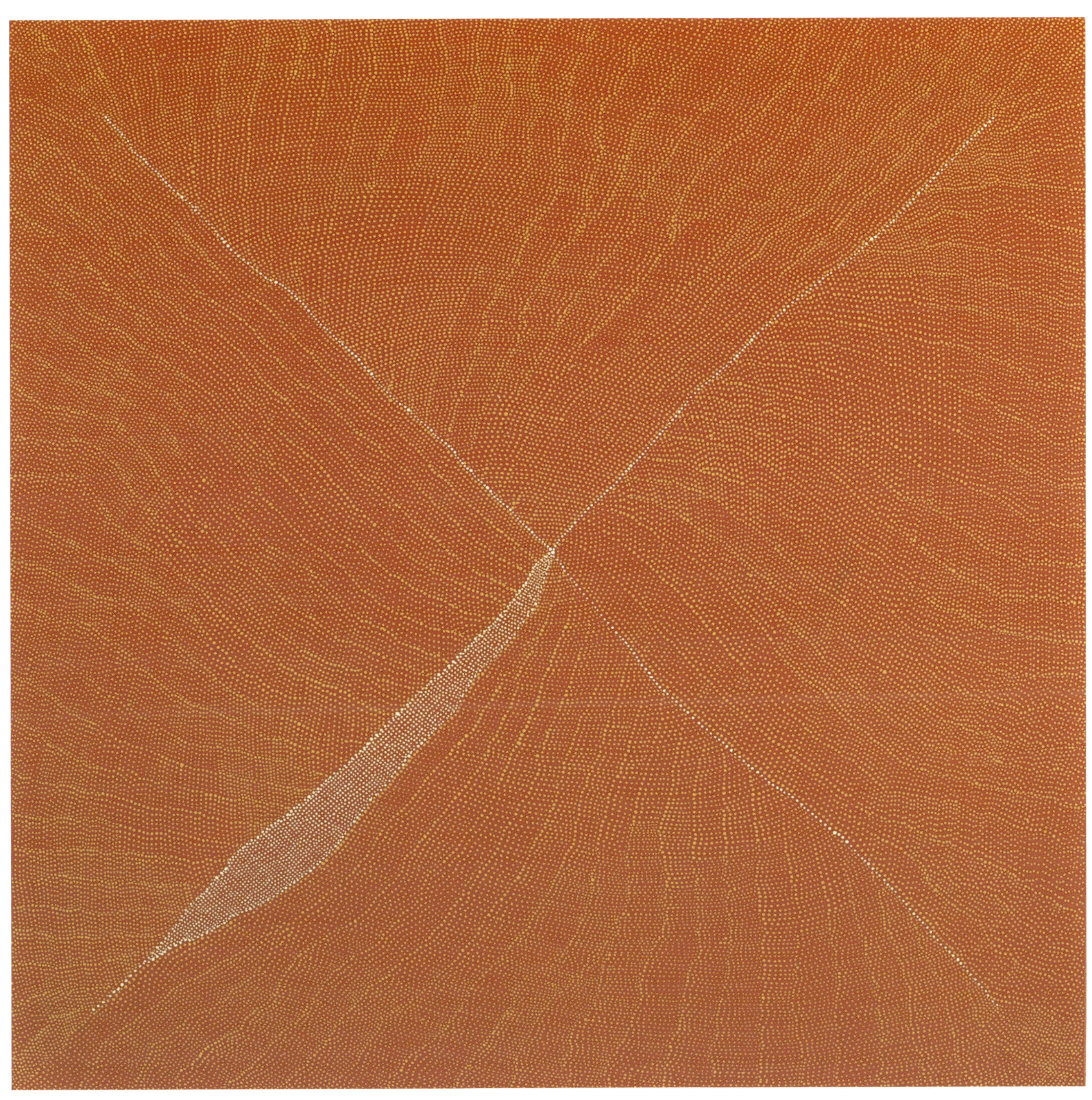

Mountain Devil Lizard Dreaming (Sandstorm) 2000 Synthetic polymer paint on Belgian linen 122 x 122 cm (4' x 4') Private collection, Woodanilling, Australia

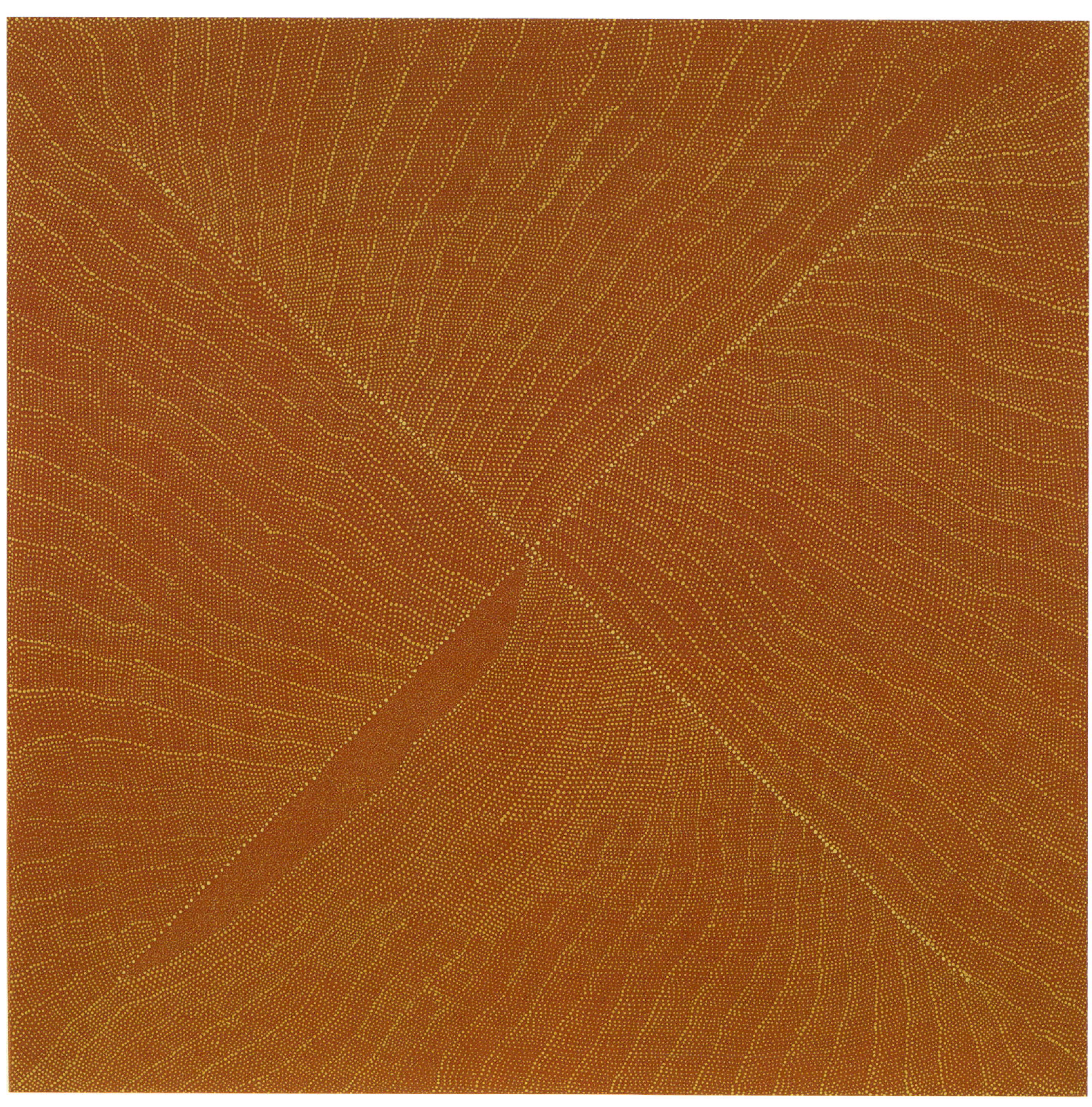

Mountain Devil Lizard Dreaming (Sandstorm) 2000 Synthetic polymer paint on Belgian linen 122 x 122 cm (4' x 4') Private collection, courtesy of Gallerie Australis, Adelaide, Australia

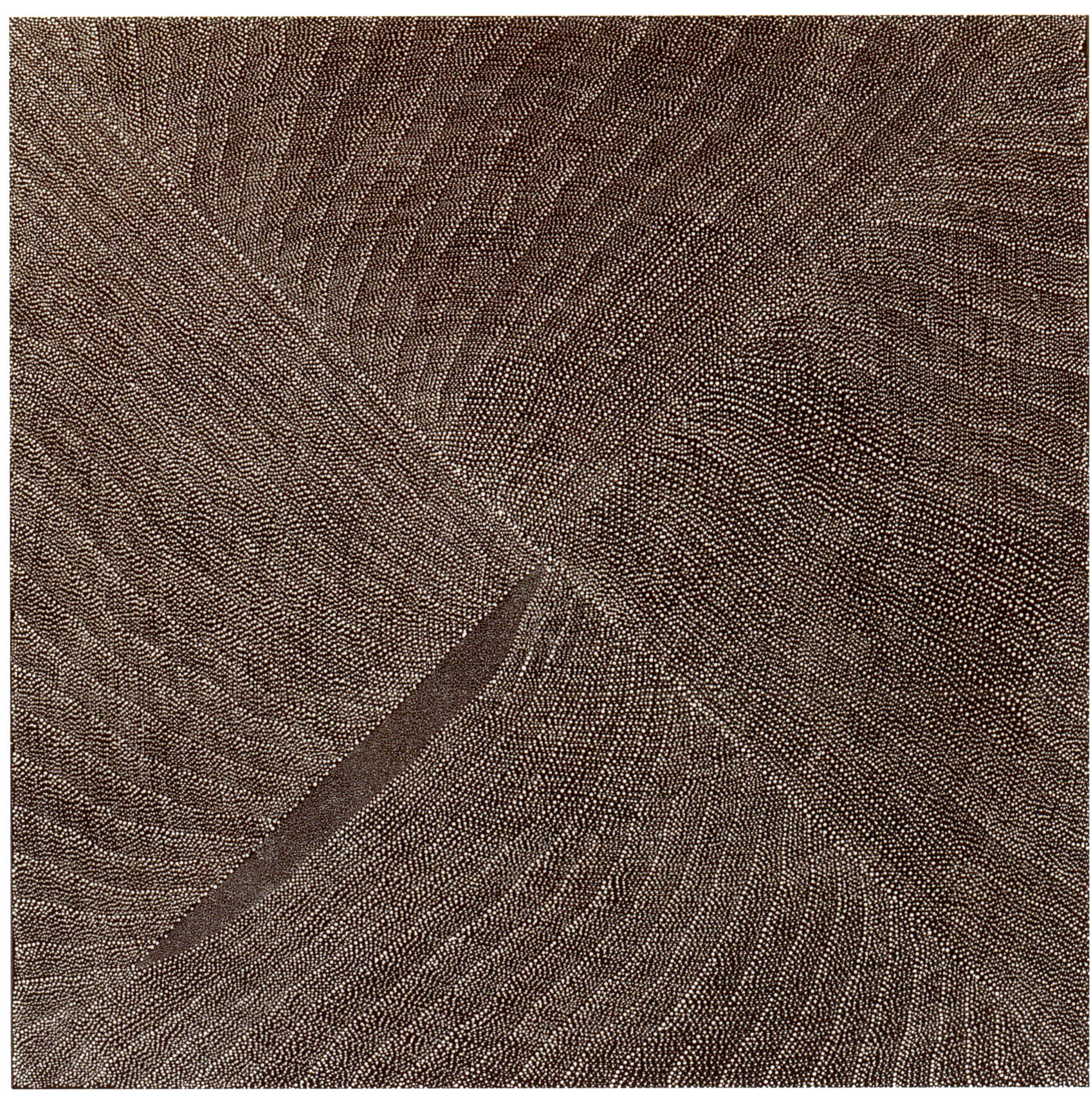

Mountain Devil Lizard Dreaming 2000 Synthetic polymer paint on Belgian linen 122 x 122 cm (4' x 4') Thomas Vroom Collection, The Netherlands

My Country – Bush Seeds 2000 Synthetic polymer paint on Belgian linen 91.5 x 91.5 cm (3' x 3') Private collection, Melbourne, Australia

My Country – Bush Seeds 2000 Synthetic polymer paint on Belgian linen 122 x 122 cm (4' x 4') Private collection, Denver, United States of America

My Country – Bush Seeds 2000 Synthetic polymer paint on Belgian linen 91 x 122 cm (3' x 4') Private collection, Melbourne, Australia

My Country – Bush Seeds (Sandstorm) 2000 Synthetic polymer paint on Belgian linen 152 x 152 cm (5' x 5') Private collection, Sydney, Australia

THE KINDNESS OF

Late afternoon, Iylenty (Mosquito Bore), Utopia, Northern Territory, 5 December 2000. Hazy, humid sky over flat mulga and spinifex country. Temperature: c. 37°C. Christine Nicholls and I lay our swags resignedly on the concrete floor of an abandoned house, one of a cluster of six or so which constitute the outstation, set in spinifex and mulga desert. One modest-sized central space including a kitchen sink and a sleeping area at either end. No power, no toilet (long grass – Joe Blakes?[1] – out the back), dirt on floor, soiled dishes and bedding strewn around, some evangelical Christian literature. It looks as if white-fellas had last camped here; perhaps there has been a death in the house, keeping Indigenous people away.[2] All the fly-screens over the windows are broken. To get a puff of air the doors will have to be left open.

Nocturnal visits by mosquitoes certain, hungry camp dogs probable, drunks, the least of our real concerns, entirely possible. It is going to be a hard three days.

Kathleen Petyarre materialises at our door. She has wandered over from her bush base, a house similar to ours 100 metres away. She sits at the entrance to catch the hope of a breeze. I give her a cup of orange juice, purchased from the Utopia Store, Ahalper, an hour earlier.[3] She says quietly, firmly: 'Too many drunks. You go and stay with Simon' (the white art co-ordinator, Simon Turner). We pack up and make the twenty-minute drive back to Ahalper, a modest scatter of houses like Iylenty, but our arrival is unexpected. Simon consults with his partner Ramona Herd, who is unwell: with good grace they take us in. We are to share a room in a house with . . . an air conditioner.

Kathleen is used to negotiating between worlds. The drunks she spoke of, in spite of community efforts to keep Utopia dry, were real enough, but she probably used them as an excuse to look after us, imagining, quite correctly, that we would have suffered under the third-world conditions her people live with as a daily reality. I had met Petyarre in Adelaide and Sydney a number of times previously. She looked far more relaxed at Utopia. It remains her country and she is still one of its bosses.

We were visiting Petyarre at her country in a small window of days snatched from our busy itineraries, not least hers. She had recently returned from Bali, where she had been working courtesy of her dealer, and was due to take up an artist's residency in New Zealand in the new year, indicators that she is no stranger to international travel. She usually resides and paints in Adelaide.

She has had little chance in recent years to spend time with her kin, but we caught up with her at Iylenty with her predominantly female family, from four-year-old grand-daughter Josie-Anne, to Maggie Pwerle, her mother of around ninety years old. She also has a camp at Atneltyey (Boundary Bore), another of the 'Utopia' outstations. Her Iylenty house is similar to the one we were to stay in. Outside it were signs of Petyarre's success: a troop carrier, BMX bikes for the kids lying amid the litter: there is nowhere to go on them. On our second day in the area, after several hours of climbing the high, red dunes most sacred to Petyarre in the searing midday heat, we were invited inside her house to shake hands with Maggie, a frail, charming and gracious old lady lying on one of the foam mattresses which cover the floor. The heat tends to make anything other than relaxing unthinkable. Petyarre's little smile bespoke welcome, pride and satisfaction.

The three tiny outstations, Iylenty, Ahalper and Atneltyey, are some 250 kilometres north-east of Alice Springs, and sit within the north-western quadrant of Utopia Station. The word 'Utopia' as a verbal umbrella for these and other neighbouring settlements, about twenty in all, sounds irresistibly ironic to Western ears. Ahalper is nonetheless host to Urapuntja Artists, one of around 55 government-sponsored, Indigenous art co-operatives, the core of the 'Aboriginal art industry' which very conservatively generates over A$100 million a year.[4] These centres in aggregate are effectively reviving the forgotten ideal of the aesthetic-as-social: in the words of one present day philosopher, 'aesthetic experience can be seen as being related to the utopian perspective of unblocked communicative relationships between . . . individuals as well as of . . . individuals with themselves'.[5] This statement suggests that reassertions the aesthetic can accord with calls for conversations of reconciliation entered with an openness to unpredictability, to theologian Martin Buber's 'moment of surprise'.[6] A new paradigm for art is emerging world-wide which offers credence to the idea of the aesthetic working cross-culturally. I will argue that this proposition – supported by recent evolutionary and psychoanalytic theories – heavily qualifies aesthetic relativism while nonetheless facilitating interchanges free from stereotyping on the basis of race or ethnicity.

The United States critic Thomas McEvilley has identified three significant breaks in Western art to date:

> One when the population of Europe was changed by the so-called barbarian invasions in the late Roman Empire, which led to the transition from Greco-Roman to Christian art; the second with the Renaissance, the transition from Christian art to European art; the third at the beginning of the twentieth century, with the transition from European to Modern art. Each of these breaks in tradition was associated with a deep infusion of foreign influence – respectively, Germanic, Byzantine and African/Oceanic.[7]

Art as we know it, self-conscious and autonomous, came into being somewhere along that lurching historical line. European art drew on Jean-Jacques Rousseau's fantasies of the visceral life of tribal communities as opposed to the vitiated life of Europe before it collapsed under the weight of self-doubt into modern art. This move was also predicated upon an exaggeration of transcendental aestheticism, inspired by Immanuel Kant's separation, in the late eighteenth century, of the cognitive, the aesthetic and the moral, accompanied by a false sense of art representing absolute values and of being above society. Art levitated beyond craft, as above any sustained consideration of the terms of its material production.

The historicist presumptions of 'modern art' – of endless progress and expanding Western hegemony – came under postmodernist counterfire in the latter decades of the last century. Many found in modernism's supposedly universal values a continuing blindness to sexism, racism and colonialism. Criticisms of the 1984 exhibition *'Primitivism' in Twentieth Century Art: Affinity of the Tribal and the Modern* at the Museum of Modern Art, New York, were a significant symptom of the ensuing turmoil. (The problem with *'Primitivism'* for McEvilley, for example, was that it sought to enfold 'tribal' art as a form of proto-modernism within the domain of supposedly timeless – read provincial Euro-American – modernist aesthetics).[8] It is no coincidence that this period was also that of the Aboriginal art renaissance. Elements of the repressed thus returned, in a climate conditioned by the three prevailing ideologies of our time, as succinctly summarised by an International Red Cross official: 'ecology, human rights and humanitarian ethics'.[9] The terms of postmodernist thinking – as the hothouse product of northern hemisphere conurbations – were nonetheless largely dictated by modernism, which precluded, for the most part, the 'far-cultural': the environment, science generally and non-Western cultures.[10]

It is not surprising, then, that confusion surrounds the 'framing' of contemporary traditional Aboriginal art, of which Petyarre's is a prime example. Her art stems from spiritual, economic and social rituals, and may thus deservedly be called religious art, in a full sense of the term. If the sway of Western representational systems means that galleries of Aboriginal art have yet to attract the audiences which throng, say, the Uffizi, the best work in both – and Aboriginal art is bound to take its place as a significant movement of twentieth-century art – comprises a particularly intense fusion of meta-physical belief, tradition and innovative form.

Petyarre's work also comprises a meta-ritual, the picturing of belief and the forms of tradition for a Western audience, using materials and marketing techniques laid down by Western advisers. The artist has executed much of her mature work in suburban Adelaide houses. Her dealer, David Cossey, provides her with primed canvases, colours and general support. Petyarre's situation constitutes a paradigm of the necessarily mediated circumstances of contemporary traditional Indigenous artists, including those at remote area art centres. It also falls within – if towards one end of – the normal spectrum of Western artist-dealer interactions.

Petyarre typically works in the company of her sister Violet, without whom she is 'lonely',[11] before a large television set, applying paint with satay sticks through the night. Her work has become progressively more carefully articulated in recent years, to the point of using string to help establish the true centre and radiating lines of some of her Mountain Devil works, for example, in response to Western taste. Petyarre thus inflects a traditional Indigenous perspective, in which 'beauty' lies in the truth of the Dreaming concerned, rather than in the outward form of its rendition. The *Arnkerrth*, for Petyarre, is central, as the bearer of survival knowledge, to women's induction rites. The landscape the little lizard battles and blends with is important for its capacities to support life and as an interactive stage for the *Arnkerrth's* heroism. The vagaries of its appearance or passing weather are much less significant, contrary to the titles of some of Petyarre's works.

Yet it is immediately apparent to the viewer that Petyarre is able to suggest a complex, energised reading of the land in its manifold dimensions – not precluding its appearance by Western reckoning – through the sophisticated application of a breathtakingly simple technique. This is well indicated in two works in the Art Gallery of South Australia.[12] In *Mountain Devil Lizard Dreaming (with winter sandstorm)*, 1996, radiating lines work across an irregular pattern of concentric circles, all formed solely from white and ochre dots on a black ground, to create the kinetic force of a Catherine wheel, induction areas at its eye; in *My country (bush seeds)*, 1998, light yellow and earth-red dots on a dark umber ground suggest lines of trees towards the top, with induction sites clustering below, for Westerners, as clouds of unknowing.

It seems that Petyarre has become increasingly less specific in her renditions of such sites, even as her more recent work, including the 'white' pictures suggesting an aeroplane view per converging parallels, indicate, literally, a Western perspective. It is not surprising that her own trajectory should veer towards the West. Like most non-Indigenous artists, Petyarre is motivated in part by a desire for fame and money (indeed an economic imperative is scarcely new to Indigenous cultural practices: in pre-contact times, for example, ceremonies of increase were traded). Petyarre wants to be as well known as her 'Auntie Emily',[13] that is, the first Aboriginal woman artist to achieve star status, the late Emily Kame Kngwarreye, who was also from Utopia. To characterise Aboriginal culture as being 'incommensurable' with Western culture, as many writers continue to state or imply, is to shade from either everyday or ethnographic perspectives to the ethnocentric.

This slippage might stem, on the part of the non-Indigenous, from a bedazzled respect, a contradiction in itself: true incommensurability would surely tend

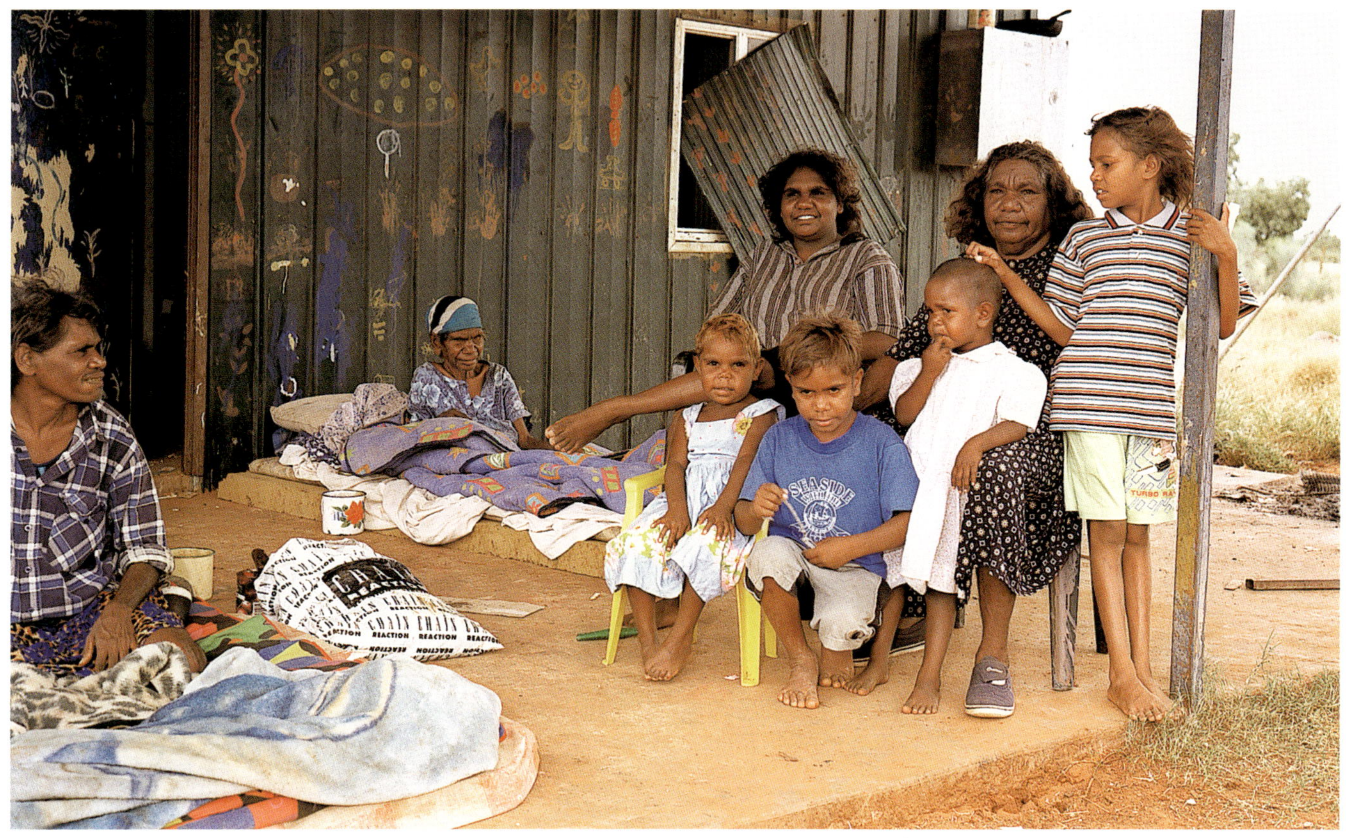

Kathleen Petyarre and relatives at Iylenty (Mosquito Bore), Utopia, Northern Territory, 6 December 2000. From left: Gracie Ngale, Maggie Pwerle (Kathleen's mother), Josie Anne Petyarre, Roseanne Petyarre (Gracie's daughter), Josiah Kemarre (nick-named 'Jo-Jay'), Gracie's grand-daughter Pwerle, Kathleen Petyarre, Sabrina Pwerle Photograph by Ian North

to leave one coldly alienated. Indigenous writers sometimes assert the idea to suggest, politically, the special character of their culture. 'The incommensurable' is too often simply a poetic substitution for 'ignorance' (which is certainly real enough). Both blacks and whites thus perpetuate the pervasive postmodern myth of 'the Other', as being necessary to one's identity but inferior to oneself, thereby confirming modernist boundaries and racist stereotyping.[14] In so doing they repudiate the complexity both of the artists' aims and of the resultant w ork. Against this, a number of significant cultural commentators have noted that assertions of incommensurablity with respect to language systems wrongly imply both the homogeneity of languages, not to mention the everyday, if problematic, fact of translation.[15] The analogy with art, a zone which generally has less need of intercultural mediation than written material, will be apparent.

Kathleen Petyarre, in common with other senior Aboriginal artists of her generation, was brought up in her country without significant contact with European culture. She therefore has particular lessons and visions to offer the rest of us, Indigenous or non-Indigenous, who have led lives less obviously grounded in the material conditions of human survival. These she has made into art, with three principal aspects: the cultural, the ecological (sourced in its subject matter and vice versa) and the aesthetic. It is this last quality, imbricated with the first two,

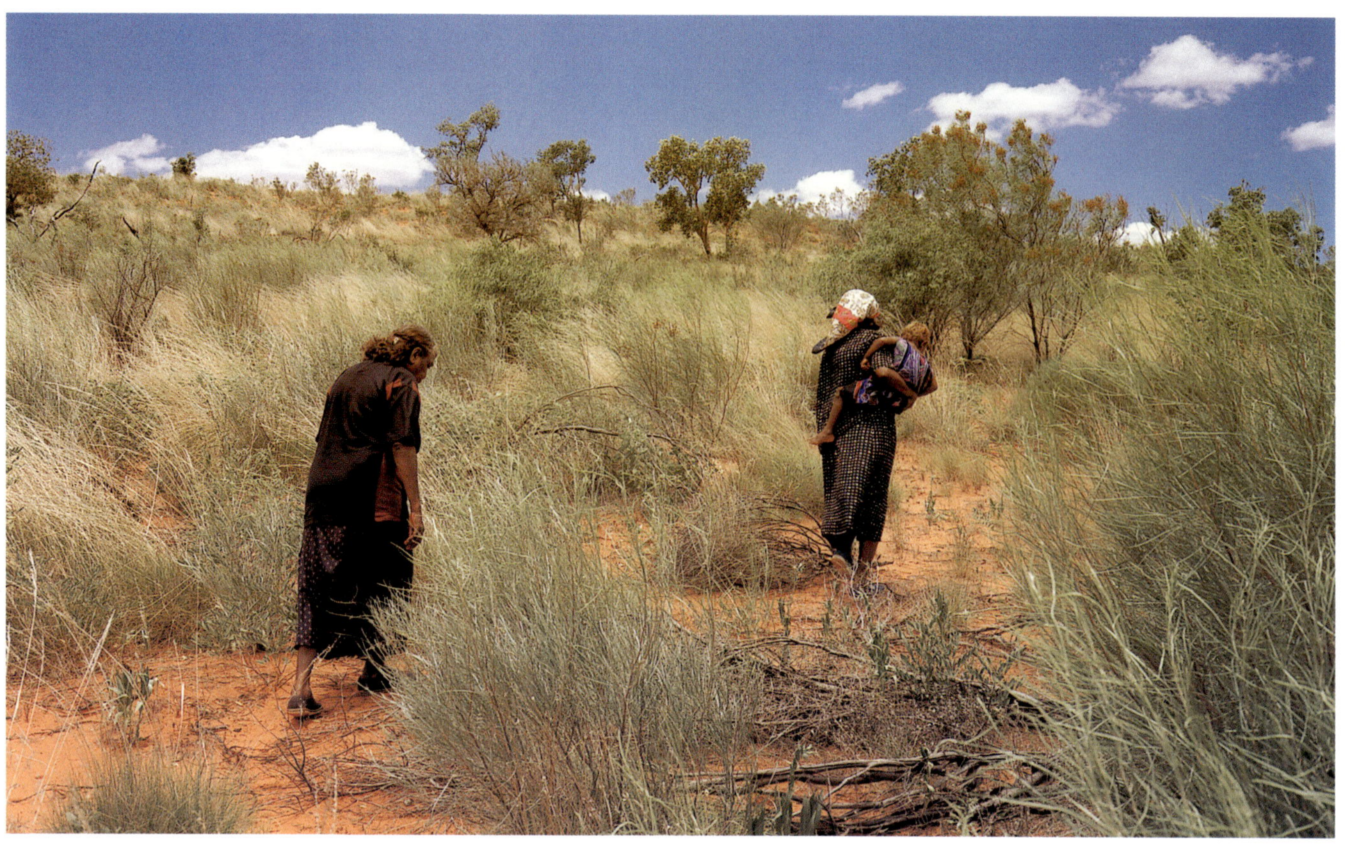

Kathleen Petyarre and Myrtle Petyarre, Kathleen's elder sister, nursing Josie Anne Petyarre, walk up the sandhill or 'mountain' as Kathleen describes it, towards the ceremonial site on Kathleen and her siblings' country, December 2000 Photograph by Ian North

which gives her work communicative power; the first two qualities animate the third. None of this is to deny the remarkable work of many non-Indigenous artists who are acknowledging the environment, for example, within a global framework.[16] But few contemporary cultures could show with greater clarity than the Aboriginal the root and basis of all cultures in the environment, a connection which surely has a pressing claim on our attention in the light of, for example, constantly re-issued warnings about global warming. Yet of the three terms identified above, it is the aesthetic, that 'anachronistic embarrassment',[17] that is the most contested today. Both McEvilley and his critic, G. Roger Denson, for example, suggest that we 'replace the conventional views of the mind, its privileging of a (falsely) innate aesthetic response with a nomadic virtuosity that allows us to examine the models that exist outside the West'.[18] But the idea of the 'universally' aesthetic and the nomadic are not as incompatible as they have even recently seemed.

The prevailing scepticism of our culture has reduced beauty to imperialism's mask, a caricature of its potentialities.[19] Yet it is as important to notice not just what a work means, but the complex poetics of *how* it means, in Petyarre's case through her prescribed Dreamings and the representational repertoire she both inherited and developed. Thinking thus is to begin recombining Kant's categories. A literary critic, Christopher Beach, has surveyed recent attempts to rehabilitate the aesthetic as an active focus of thought by positing it, variously, in socio-ethical, materialist (neo-Marxist), or postmodern terms.[20] (These approaches clearly go beyond the traditional, highly restrictive idea of aesthetics as rules for beauty.) Each of these variously problematic categories seems relevant to Indigenous art, as this essay may so far have implied, even if Beach cautions that 'these attempts to rescue the aesthetic through . . . metaesthetic means seem less convincing than theoretical and practical discussions of the aesthetic object itself'.[21]

The latter approach might encourage the appreciation of the fine differences in quality and approach over the span of Petyarre's oeuvre, the subtle intensity of her best works, and the dangers she faces of overproduction and in being separated for long spells from her country.[22] It would also allow us to see the political in the primarily apolitical, allowing that art possesses agency in ways which are far from obvious, even in the face of the greatest horrors. As Beach stated of the German philosopher Theodor Adorno, 'despite his much-quoted statement that it is no longer possible to write [lyric] poetry after Auschwitz – no longer possible to engage in the same kind of aesthetic activity as before the war – [he] believed that a continuing examination of all forms of cultural production, including the aesthetic dimension . . . was more necessary than ever'[23] once the machinery of genocide was halted. Adorno postwar advocated the cause of 'non-committed' (apolitical) art and eschewed the cheaply moralistic, because any art which derived its terms from a corrupt culture was bound, itself, to be compromised. In Petyarre's powerful, aesthetic work, her *alter ego*, the *Arnkerrth*, also speaks as a survivor. Her work takes on a political dimension in reaffirming, indirectly but clearly, her people's connection to their land.

To consider art's manifold dimensions is to adopt both the anthropologist's etic (from the outside) and emic (from the inside) perspectives simultaneously. The adoption of Aboriginal motifs by non-Indigenous Australian artists c. 1940–1970, that is, in the period immediately preceding the Aboriginal art renaissance, had a bearing on preparing non-Indigenous Australian appreciation of Aboriginal art.[24] More generally, Aboriginal art seems to fill a gap: it looks familiar to anyone acquainted with modernist abstraction. (This association does not necessarily work easily in either direction. Petyarre viewed a Rosalie Gascoigne work of heat-buckled plywood or galvanised iron as 'rubbish': it perhaps seemed too close to building detritus at Utopia.[25]) Indigenous art, however, stems, from a pre-modern, indeed prehistorical culture, so it appears to mainline into values largely lost to the West. The work has the aura created by its beauty and the second-order aura of its religious prestige: the gap between engagement with the work and lack of knowledge about the culture behind can magnify the effect of both.[26] They may thus combine, in the anthropomorphic words of cultural theorist Walter Benjamin in 1939, to create the effect of an artwork looking back at the viewer from a quasi 'ceremonial', awe-inspiring distance,[27] even as it fills our close attention.

There is something here of aesthetician Elaine Scarry's recent, neo-Platonic characterisation of beauty as a 'compact' between viewer and object,[28] for example, and James Kirwan's more penetrating idea of beauty as a double movement of the psyche – an unconscious echo of Benjamin, perhaps – a simultaneous projection of desire and repression of awareness that the process is occurring.[29] Kirwan's view is analogous to the psychoanalytic theory of transference, wherein the analysand projects his or her fantasies onto a neutral analyst within (to the latter) an alienated relationship. The recently promoted concept of empathy is more productive for psychoanalysis, it seems, and has pertinent implications for art. It suggests that 'receptacles of projection', to work as such and whether human or not, have to possess particular attributes, which are informed by both culture and, ultimately, evolution. To accept this is to re-admit the possibility, at least, of (near) universally applicable aesthetic characteristics, however culturally inflected,[30] as a common basis of communication between, for instance, artist and viewer.

It is also to help one theorise the idea of an empathic resonance with an artwork, and, by

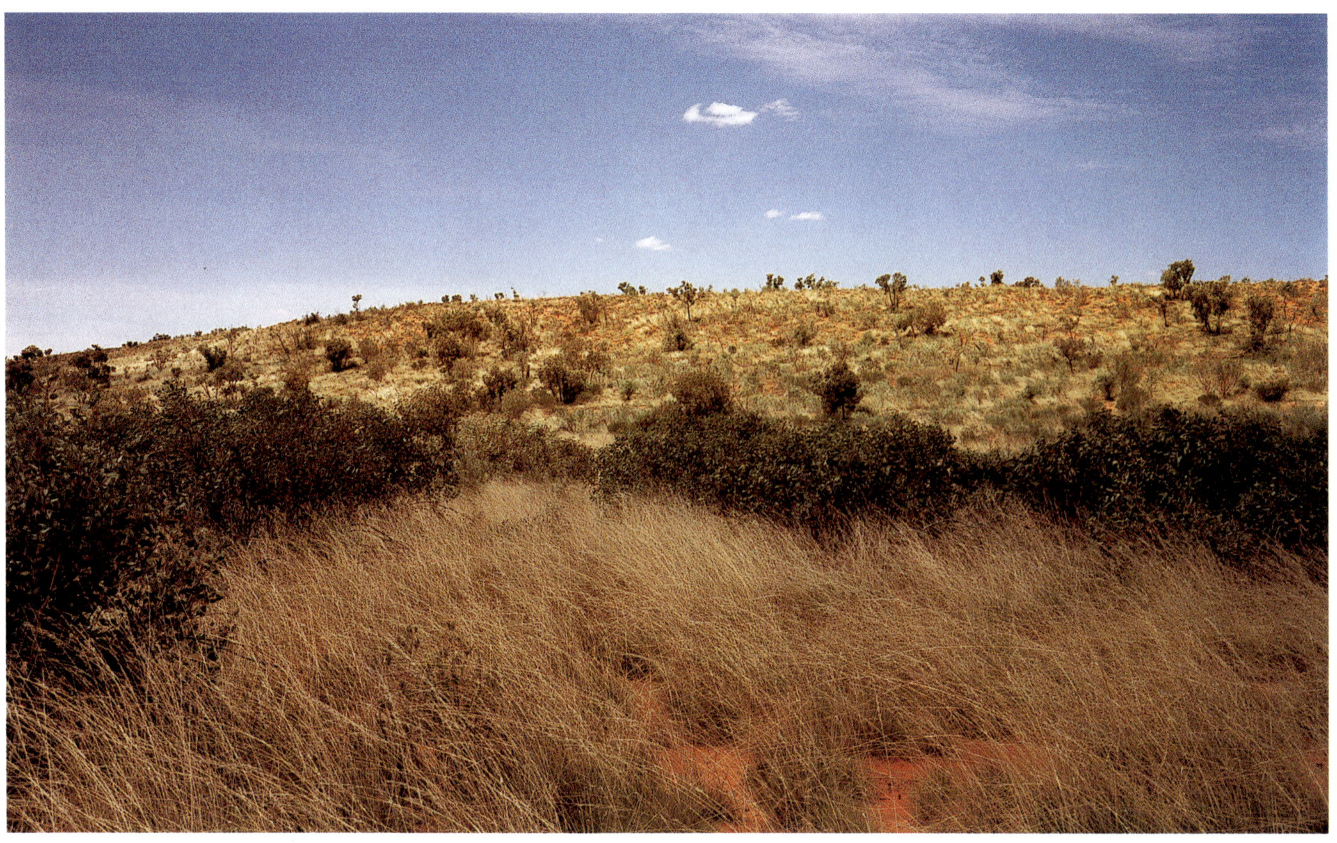

Looking towards sandhill on approach to ceremonial site, Atnangker country, Northern Territory, December 2000 Photograph by Ian North

extension, a culture. By Russell Meares's account, a sense of self is generated by an internal conversation between two inner languages, one of associative, memory-dependent and image-filled thought, the other linear, practical and purposeful, developed for dealing with the outer world: in popular but misleading parlance, a 'real' self and a 'false' self respectively.[31] A feeling of intimacy 'depends on the development of inner experience, which can be with another'[32] (and not necessarily an intimate in the everyday sense, but rather, anyone with whom one can share emotionally significant thoughts, images or memories, in a state of well-being. It is important that the other here, unlike the 'postmodern Other', must be perceived as an *equal*, in terms of vulnerability). Trauma can block the memories on which intimacy depends: therapy depends on their resurrection through the 're-creation of the doubleness of self through the resonance of the other'.[33] It would seem possible to extrapolate from individual psychotherapy to cultural communication: a sense of resonant connection with 'the other', far from being impossible, may be achieved (*inter alia*) through aesthetic means, broadly defined, to the psychic advantage of all concerned. The 'other' may, by this extension, step over 'far-cultural' boundaries to become 'an intimate'.

But how universal are these aesthetic means? Here we might look to developments in the nascent discipline of bioaesthetics, regarding the gene-culture coevolution of our pattern-recognising, metaphor-forming brains, as outlined, for example, by the noted biologist Edward O. Wilson.[34] Art, by his account, filled (and fills) the gap between information overload as a function of expanding human intelligence, and

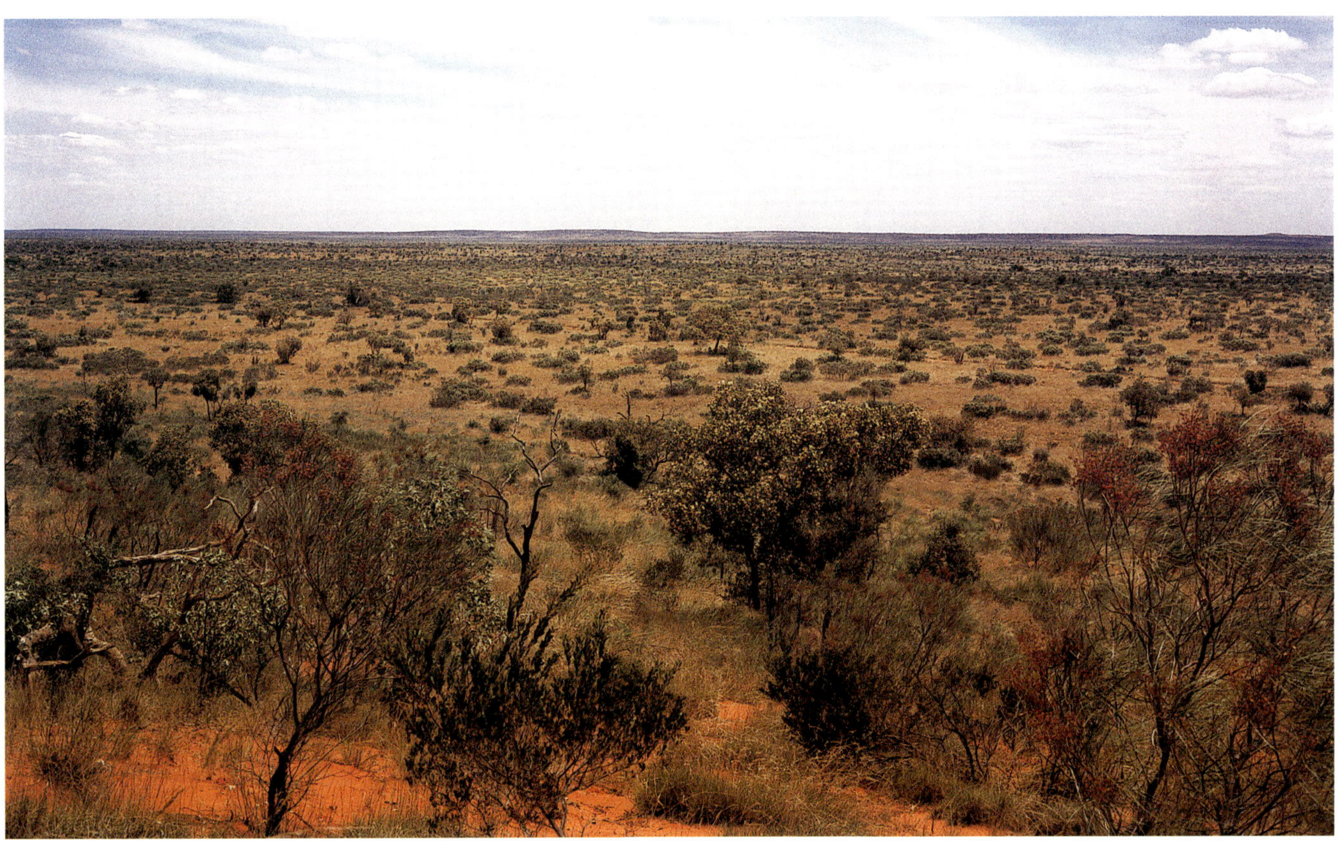

Atnangker country from the ceremonial site, Northern Territory, December 2000 Photograph by Ian North

developing epigenetic algorithms, or rules, of 'human nature': as part of evolution of human culture 'universals or near universals emerged'.[35] Evolutionary and psychoanalytic theory may help us move on from a cultural studies perspective, as exemplified by Beach, as from Western cultural narcissism.[36] As if to frame Petyarre's work, Wilson notes that both hunter-gatherers and urbanites are 'aware of fewer than one in a thousand of the kinds of organisms . . . that sustain the ecosystems around them', and that :

> Through cumulative science in a literate world . . . the archaic world of myth and passion is perceived as it truly is, across the full range of cause and effect. Every contour of the terrain, every plant and animal living in it, and the human intellect that masters them all, can be understood more completely as a physical entity. Yet in so doing we have not abandoned the instinctual world of our ancestors. By focusing on the peculiarly human niche in the continuum, we can if we wish . . . inhabit all the productions of art with [a] sense of beauty and mastery . . . no barrier stands between the material world of science and the sensibilities of the hunter and the poet.[37]

We are free, then, to dig deeper the 'human well of imagination' which Denson saw – in spite of doubts about universal forms of signification – as the source of 'all inspiration and imagination'.[38]

None of this is to deny the desirability of investigating, with the literary theorist Susan Stewart, ways in which 'aesthetic modalities', especially the lyric – 'the querying of the boundary between the somatic and the social' – correspond to the situation artists face under the historical pressure of dislocating cultural processes.[39] Recasting the somatic as the aesthetic, we can see that such forces have increasingly impelled Kathleen Petyarre to claim a place as an artist within Western as well as classical Aboriginal culture, her measured lyricism the product of a dialectic between her own traditions and Western ways of picturing. Petyarre's studio *modus operandi*, described above, indicates not only the characteristic, basic mechanics of Indigenous and Western art intersection, but also how Western audience expectations – encouraged by an unprecedented acceptance of Aboriginal culture and a hunger for the aesthetic alike – feed back into her work. But if the artist is buoyed by a consequent sense of pride, she is motivated rather by a need to communicate her knowledge, her culture and her vision, as a species of kindness (or so it can seem to its recipients), offered with the same benevolent authority with which she helped Christine Nicholls and myself at Utopia.

A similar motive perhaps led Petyarre to allow a white man, her former partner, Ray Beamish, to work with her on her paintings at one point – a gesture mixed, no doubt, with a sensible willingness to accept assistance for the more tedious aspects of painting, like infill dotting. This led to an unnecessary controversy over authorship, the instigators of which failed to notice sufficiently either the manifest qualities of Petyarre's solo work or the Aboriginal tradition of such collaboration, to which the idea of kindness, augmenting culturally mandated giving, is perhaps not irrelevant. Petyarre is obliged by Aboriginal law to guard and communicate her Dreamings, as the expression of cultural needs based on desert survival. The word 'kindness' necessarily acquires quotation marks in this context, a point to underscore. To some extent, it is just a fortunate co-incidence for the wider world that Western infrastructure fell into place as the artist reached her maturity. Yet Petyarre is also kind: not so much gentle-kind – she is nothing if not a robust survivor – as redemptively benevolent beyond the ego-bound pleasures of generosity. The simple truth is that she is not obliged to share her Dreamings as widely as she does. She thus contributes to a growing Euro-Australian perception that Indigenous peoples are responding to more than two centuries of oppression with a collective act of cultural grace.

Kathleen Petyarre's personal kindness and her cultural giving are linked, the first suggesting that empathy can make the second viable. In combination they make her an active participant in a paradigm shift towards a global art – which, to paraphrase a multicultural slogan, should mean not homogenisation but diversity within equality – slowly evolving world-wide,[40] in the face of growing divisions between rich and poor across, rather than reflecting, national, ethnic and cultural lines.[41] Petyarre's painting helps constitute this new situation, the terms of which lend it an aspect of its value. But this accrues principally from her work's manifest qualities. It is impossible to separate the aesthetic from the socio-political framework of its production. This Petyarre's work shares with all art, yet like all good art it makes its own place in the world. Step back, and Petyarre's work is a tile in a vast, developing mosaic of global equilateralism, whereby the certainties and scepticism of modernism and postmodernism are giving way to reconciliation, a sense of intercultural respect. Step forward. One may receive an epiphanic gift.

Acknowledgements

I wish to acknowledge Christine Nicholls, for freely sharing her knowledge of Indigenous culture in general and of Petyarre's life and work in particular; and also Henry Krystall, for information on current psychoanalytic theory. Both commented usefully on an earlier draft of this essay, as did Daniel Thomas: my thanks to them all, as to Katherine Leeson for editing assistance.

Notes

1 Snakes.

2 I am following the developing convention of using a capital 'I' for Indigenous, which, like the long-standing convention of 'Aboriginal', signifies Indigenous people of Australia, as opposed to indigenous or aboriginal inhabitants elsewhere.

3 The store is also known, signposted and registered as the 'Arlparra Store'; the term comes from 'Ahalper', which is the currently preferred

spelling for the name of the surrounding country and the neighbouring settlement (email from Jenny Green, 18 February 2001).

4 David Langsam, 'Aboriginal Art: Australia's hidden resource', *Art Monthly Australia*, March 1996: 10. See also Felicity Wright and Frances Morphy (eds.), *The Art & Craft Centre Story* (2 vols.) (Canberra: Aboriginal and Torres Strait Islander Commission, 1999).

5 Albrecht Wellmer, cited by Christopher Beach, 'Recuperating the Aesthetic', in James Soderholm (ed.), *Beauty and the Critic* (Tuscaloosa and London: University of Alabama Press, 1997), 106.

6 Raimond Gaita, 'The Rite Stuff', *Australian's Review of Books*, 1998, Vol. 3, Issue 9: 13. Cf. Martin Buber, *I and Thou* (1937) (Edinburgh: T. & T. Clark, 1970), 67: 'The You encounters me by grace – it cannot be found by seeking . . . the You encounters me. But I enter into a direct relationship to it'.

7 Thomas McEvilley, 'Doctor, Lawyer, Indian Chief', in McEvilley (with G. Roger Denson), *Capacity: History, the World, and the Self in Contemporary Art Criticism* (Amsterdam: G+B Arts International, 1966), 117.

8 *Ibid.*, esp. 111–112.

9 Gilbert Holleufer, cited in Michael Ignatieff, *The Warrior's Honour* (London: Vintage, 1999), 156.

10 To expand the reach of the term as used by G. Roger Denson, 'The World and its Difference', in McEvilley, *Capacity*, 96. Denson was referring only to non-Western cultures.

11 As stated by Petyarre to the author, Adelaide, 12 March 2001.

12 *Mountain Devil Lizard Dreaming (with winter sandstorm)*. 1996. Synthetic polymer paint on canvas, 183 x 183 cm., accession number 967P104; *My Country (bush seeds)*. 1998. Synthetic polymer paint on Belgian linen, 244 x 244 cm., accession number 996P29.

13 Kathleen Petyarre, in unpublished interview with Christine Nicholls, Bali, September–October 2000.

14 Cf. Rasheed Araeen, 'The Art of Benevolent Racism', *Third Text*, no. 51 (Summer 2000): esp. 59, 62–63.

15 e.g. Bob Hodge, 'Aboriginal Iconographies of Home', *Communal/ Plural*, 5 (1997): 48; Ihab Hassan, '"How Australian is it?"' *Australian Book Review* (September 2000): 34.

16 e.g. see Ian North, *Expanse: Aboriginalities, Spatialities and the Politics of Ecstasy* (Adelaide: University of South Australia Art Museum, 1998), the catalogue for an exhibition which included Petyarre alongside the non-Indigenous artists Jon Cattapan, Rosalie Gascoigne, Antony Hamilton and Imants Tillers. See also an account of the work of Joan Brassil in Susan Best, 'You are now on Aboriginal land', in *Pre/dictions: the Role of Art at the End of the Millennium: Proceedings of the Art Association of Australia and New Zealand held in Wellington, 2–5 December 1999*, ed. Jenny Harper (Wellington: Victoria University, 2000), 18–25.

17 Fredric Jameson, *Late Marxism: Adorno, or, the Persistence of the Dialectic* (London and New York: Verso, 1990), 129.

18 Denson, 'Reincarnations and Visitations: Modernism and Post-modernism all Over Again', in McEvilley, *Capacity*, 218.

19 As captured in the ironic title of Eric Michaels's noteworthy essay 'Bad Aboriginal Art', *Art & Text*, 28 (March–May 1988): 59–73.

20 Beach, 'Recuperating', 96–97; 106–107.

21 *Ibid.*, 106.

22 The problems of over-production and increasing divorce from original sources of inspiration are common to both Indigenous and non-Indigenous artists reliant on the Western gallery system for their principal income.

23 Beach, 107.

24 See Clare Baddeley (ed.), *Motif & Meaning: Aboriginal Influences in Australian Art 1930–1970* (Ballarat: Ballarat Fine Art Gallery, 1999).

25 Kathleen Petyarre, in an unpublished interview with Christine Nicholls at the exhibition *Expanse* (see footnote 16 above), Adelaide, 3 September, 1998. The Gascoigne works concerned were *Outback II*, 1996, *Frontiers I,II, IV*, 1998, and *Frontier V*, 1998 (illustrated in North, *Expanse*, 19).

26 Cf. Sally Butler, 'The Role of Aura at the End of the Millennium', in Harper (ed.), Pre/dictions, 46; and J.M. Coetzee, 'The Marvels of Walter Benjamin', section 2 <http://www.nybooks.com/nyrev/> posted 11 January 2001.

27 Walter Benjamin, 'On Some Motifs in Baudelaire' (1939), in Hannah Arendt (ed.), *Illuminations: Walter Benjamin* (London: Fontana, 1979), 190.

28 Elaine Scarry, *On Beauty and Being Just* (Princeton: Princeton University Press, 1999), 90.

29 James Kirwan, *Beauty* (Manchester and New York: Manchester University Press, 1999), esp. 11, 46. Cf. Benjamin,'Motifs', 190.

30 Cf. Edward O. Wilson, *Consilience: the Unity of Knowledge* (New York: Alfred A. Knopf, 1998), 217: 'universals or near universals emerged in the evolution of culture'. Cf. also John D. Barrow, *The Artful Universe* (Oxford: Clarendon Press, 1995).

31 The famed psychotherapist D.W. Winnicott also used these terms. Meares's theory appears to echo distantly, yet also constructively advance upon, Jean-Francois Lyotard's famously postmodern theory of 'incommensurable phrase regimes' reflecting cognitive or sensuous experience, a view which led to extreme scepticism about the possibility of, say, ethico-political justice.

32 Russell Meares, *Intimacy and Alienation: Memory, Trauma and Personal Being* (London and Philadelphia: Routledge, 2000), 2.

33 *Ibid.*, 4.

34 Wilson, esp. 214–237.

35 *Ibid.*, 217.

36 Cf. Meares, *Intimacy and Alienation*, 141–145.

37 Wilson, 236–237.

38 Denson, 'World and its Difference', 98.

39 Susan Stewart, 'The State of Cultural Theory and the Future of Literary Form', *Profession*, 1993: 14. (Cf. Beach, 'Recuperating,' 101–102, 106–107).

40 I have elsewhere suggested 'StarAboriginality' as a provisional term for this situation as it applies in Australia ('StarAboriginality' in Charles Green (ed.), *Postcolonial + Art: Where Now?* Critical Issues Series vol. 5 (Sydney: Artspace Visual Arts Centre, forthcoming 2001).

41 See e.g. Anatol Ieven, 'The Second Fall', Prospect, January 2001, accessed 14 February 2001 at <http://www.prospect-magazine.co.uk/ >).

GLOSSARY, MAP AND FURTHER NOTES

akngananentye (Eastern Anmatyerr): 'owner' of a tract of land and Dreamings passed down from the father's side. Kathleen Petyarre is ***akngananentye*** or an 'owner' of *Arnkerrth*, the Mountain or Thorny Devil Dreaming, in this way.

Altyerr: an Eastern Anmatyerr word for 'Dreaming'.

Anmatyerr: Kathleen Petyarre's language group and also that of her people, whose homelands are located approximately 270 kilometres north-east of Alice Springs, and also west of the Highway in the Northern Territory of Australia (see map for location of Utopia which is situated on Anmatyerr land). Petyarre is a speaker of Eastern Anmatyerr.

Arnkerrth: Eastern Anmatyerr word for Mountain Devil, *Moloch horridus*, syn. 'Thorny Devil', Kathleen Petyarre's Dreaming and totem.

Arrernte: thriving Central Australian language, with several thousand speakers living in or near Alice Springs, Northern Territory (see map). Arrernte, Anmatyerr and Alyawarr are languages of the Arandic group in Central Australia.

Atnangker – Kathleen Petyarre's birthplace, and 'country' (see map).

awely (or ***awelye***): Anmatyerr word for the women's ceremonies and ritual designs which involve painting the body, dancing and singing the appropriate songs which accompany those ritual designs/ Dreamings.

'business': Aboriginal English term used by traditionally orientated Aboriginal people throughout Australia to describe Aboriginal religious ceremonies and practices. Often the genders practise 'separate business', i.e. *'men's business'* and *'women's business'*.

Dreaming: the central tenet of Anmatyerr and Alyawarr religious belief: the Dreaming, the time of the ancestral heroes, the Law. Note that different language groups have different words for this central tenet of Aboriginal religious belief upon which Aboriginal art is based. People 'own' or 'manage' Dreamings either as an inheritance from their fathers and grandfathers or from their mothers.

Iylenty: the Anmatyerr name for Mosquito Bore, where Kathleen lives with her family when she is at home in the Northern Territory (see map).

kinship system: the system of relationships traditionally accepted by a particular culture and the rights and obligations which they involve (*Macquarie Dictionary*, 1981). Aboriginal kinship systems differ markedly from the Anglo-European system, especially in so far as they extend beyond actual or biological 'blood' relationships to classificatory relationships. In practice this means that every Anmatyerr person is related to every other Anmatyerr person.

kwertengerl (Anmatyerr language): 'owner' of a tract of land from the mother's side. Anmatyerr distinguish between landowners from the mother's and the father's side.

ntang: edible seeds from certain plants (Anmatyerr language).

nyterrm: green, or bush, bean (Eastern Anmatyerr language, one of Kathleen Petyarre's Dreamings).

orthography: Note that the standardised systems for writing specific Australian (i.e. Aboriginal) languages has changed greatly over the contact years. This particularly applies to prescribed systems of spelling and in some cases to the application of diacritical marks. Australian languages have been subject to numerous orthographies. Examples of different spellings of the same word include: Anmatyerr, Anmatyerr, Anmajirra and Apetyarr for the name of the language 'Anmatyerr'; and Petyarr, Petyarre, Pichara, Pijarra for the skin-name 'Petyarr'. In this work Kathleen Petyarre's preferred orthography for the spelling of skin-names has been used. This means that there are a number of inconsistencies in the text. See the following skin-names table for what is currently accepted by most speakers as the most up to date Anmatyerr orthography for spellings of skin-names.

outstation (homeland): (usually) small communities or family groups some distance away from a main settlement and situated on the traditional homelands belonging to a particular group. Usually people return to outstations to pursue a tradition-oriented lifestyle, often involving ceremonial activity and painting. Utopia, however, is made up entirely of a number of outstations.

'skin-name': probably a corruption of the English 'kin name'. The skin-name is the dominant form of address in Australian (i.e. Aboriginal) languages. Kathleen's 'skin-name' is 'Petyarre'. The term could be glossed as the sociolinguistic means by which traditionally oriented Indigenous Australian people express their personal, social and spiritual orientation towards other Indigenous (and on occasion, non-Indigenous) people with whom they interact and communicate. When Indigenous people pass away, for a time they may only be referred to via the skin-name. Skin-names indicate not only biological relationships between people, but also classificatory relationships, which in turn act as the template for an extensive network of social obligations. In effect, this means that all members of Anmatyerr and Alyawarr society are related to one another, regardless of biological ties, and these classificatory relationships determine their social relationships.

'tribe': the former name used for an aggregate or a social group of Australian Aboriginal people, now largely rejected by Indigenous Australians because of its earlier association with concepts of savagery and 'the primitive'. 'Clan group', 'language group', 'social group' or 'nation' (after the Native American example) are now increasingly gaining currency in its place.

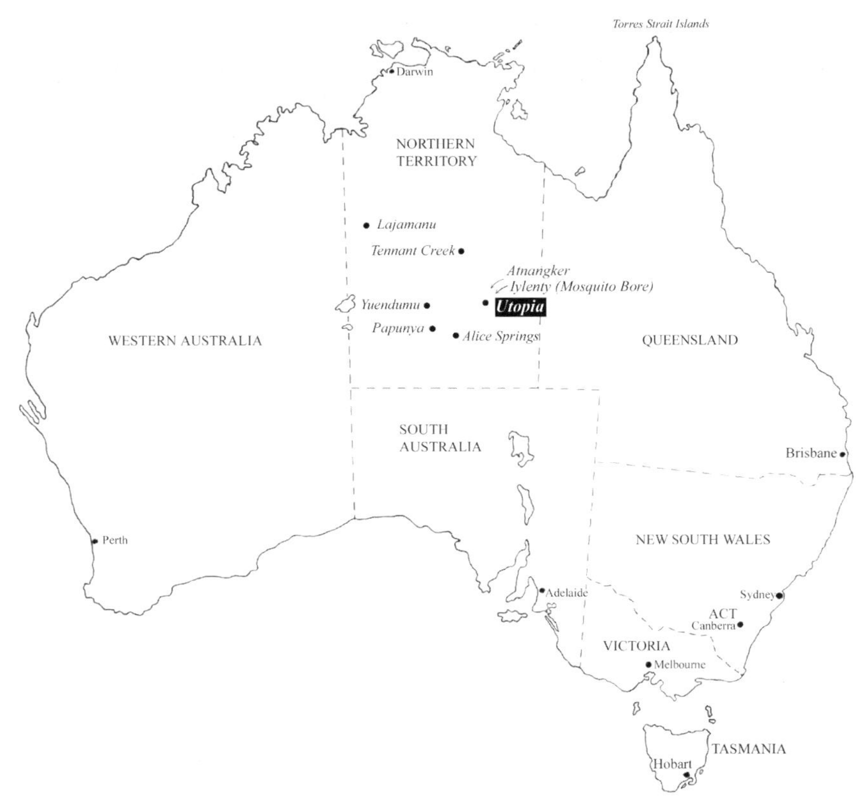

Map of Australia showing sites referred to in *Genius of Place* Courtesy of Maggie Fletcher, Flinders University Art Museum, in collaboration with Christine Nicholls

Skin-names table

Skin-names in some Arandic languages, courtesy of Jenny Green, with minor adaptations by Christine Nicholls. Note that there are a number of orthographic inconsistencies in the spellings of skin-names in this book, owing to Kathleen's preference for an older orthography for skin names. The authors feel that it is important to abide by the wishes of the person who is the subject of this book.

Alyawarr	Central and Eastern Arrernte	Eastern Anmatyerr	Rough pronunciation guide to Arandic skin names	Comment (by Christine Nicholls)
Apetyarr	Peltharre	Apetyarr Petyarr	A-PITCH-ARA	Kathleen's skin name, and that of her sisters,formerly spelled 'Petyarre'
	Pengarte	Pengart	PUNG-ART-A	
Akemarr	Kemarre	Akemarr Kemarr	A-COME-ARA	
	Ampetyane Mpetyane	Ampetyan Mpetyan	UHM-BID-JAHN-A	
Kngwarrey Ngwarrey	Kngwarraye	Kngwarray Ngwarray	NWAR-EYE	Skin name of Kathleen's late aunt Emily, formerly spelled 'Kngwarreye'
	Penangke	Penangk	PUN-UNG-GAH	
Pwerl	Perrurle	Pwerl	PULL-AH	Skin name of Kathleen's mother and daughter, formerly spelled 'Pwerle'
	Angale	Angal Ngal	UNG-A-LAH	

KATHLEEN PETYARRE

CURRICULUM VITAE

Solo Exhibitions

1996 • *Kathleen Petyarre - Storm in Aknangkere Country*, Alcaston House Gallery, Melbourne, Victoria, Australia, 29 March-19 April

1998 • *Arnkerrthe - My Dreaming*, Alcaston Gallery, Melbourne, Victoria, Australia, 24 July-15 August

1999 • *Recent Paintings by Kathleen Petyarre*, Gallerie Australis in association with Coo-ee Gallery, Mary Place Gallery, Sydney, New South Wales, Australia, 4-21 November

2000 • *Landscape: Truth and Beauty*, Recent Paintings by Kathleen Petyarre, Alcaston Gallery, Melbourne, Victoria, Australia, 16 November-6 December

2001 • *Genius of Place: The Work of Kathleen Petyarre*, Survey Exhibition, Museum of Contemporary Art, Sydney, New South Wales, Australia, 9 May-22 July

• *Kathleen Petyarre - New Paintings*, Gallerie Australis in association with Coo-ee Gallery, Mary Place Gallery, Sydney, New South Wales, Australia 3-16 September

Group Exhibitions

1980 • *Utopia Batik*, Mona Byrne's Artworks Gallery, Diorama Village, Alice Springs, Northern Territory, Australia, no date available

• *Floating Forests of Silk: Utopia Batik From the Desert*, Adelaide Festival Centre, Adelaide, Australia, no date available

1989 • *Utopia Women's Paintings: The First Works on Canvas, A Summer Project*, S.H. Ervin Gallery, Sydney, New South Wales, Australia, 14 April-21 May

• *Utopia Women's Paintings: The First Works on Canvas, A Summer Project*, Orange Regional Gallery, Orange, New South Wales, Australia, 12 October-25 November

• *Utopia Women*, Coventry Gallery, Paddington, Sydney, New South Wales, Australia, 24 October-22 November

• *Utopia - A Picture Story, 88 Silk Batiks from the Robert Holmes à Court Collection*, Tandanya Aboriginal Cultural Institute, Adelaide, South Australia, Australia, October, 1 October-18 February 1990

1990 • *CAMMA/Utopia Artists in Residence Project*, The Perth Institute of Contemporary Art, Perth, Western Australia, Australia, 8 June-8 July

• *Utopia - A Picture Story, 88 Silk Batiks from the Robert Holmes à Court Collection*, The Royal Hibernian Academy, Dublin, Ireland, 21 August-7 September

• *Utopia - A Picture Story, 88 Silk Batiks from the Robert Holmes à Court Collection*, The Crawford Municipal Art Gallery, Cork, Ireland, Limerick City, Gallery of Art, Ireland, 13 September-1 October

• *Contemporary Aboriginal Art from The Robert Holmes a Court Collection*, Carpenter Centre for the Visual Arts Harvard University, Boston, Massachusetts, United States of America, 22 February-25 March

• *Contemporary Aboriginal Art from The Robert Holmes à Court Collection*, James Ford Bell Museum, University of Minnesota, United States of America, 20 April-2 June

• *Contemporary Aboriginal Art from The Robert Holmes à Court Collection*, Lakewood Centre for the Arts, Lake Oswego, United States of America, 15 June-19 July

1994 • *Utopia Mixed Exhibition - Festival of Arts*, Gallerie Australis, Adelaide, South Australia, Australia, March-April

• *The Evolving Dreamtime: Contemporary Art by Indigenous Australians from the Kelton Foundation Collection*, Pacific Asia Art Museum in Pasadena, California, United States of America, 3 August

1996 • *Artists from Ngukurr, Haasts Bluff & Utopia*, Gallerie Australis, Adelaide, South Australia, Australia, 9-28 February

• *The Third National Aboriginal & Torres Strait Islander Heritage Commission Art Award*, Canberra, Australian Capital Territory, Australia, 2 April

• *14th NATSIAA Touring Exhibition*, Museums and Art Galleries of the Northern Territory, Darwin, Northern Territory, Australia, 17 August-19 October

• *14th NATSIAA Touring Exhibition*, Westpac Gallery, Melbourne, Victoria, Australia, 13 November-14 December

• *Dreamings of the Desert*, Art Gallery of South Australia, Adelaide, South Australia, Australia, 15 December-16 February 1997

1997 • *14h NATSIAA Touring Exhibition*, Gold Coast City Art Gallery, Surfers Paradise, Queensland, Australia, 18 April-17 May

• *14th NATSIAA Touring Exhibition*, Drill Hall Gallery, Canberra, Australian Capital Territory, Australia, 29 May-29 June

• *14th NATSIAA Touring Exhibition*, Campbelltown Gallery, New South Wales, Australia, 19 September-25 October

• *A Classic Collection of Aboriginal Art*, Fire-Works Gallery, Brisbane, Queensland, Australia, June

• *Schilderijen uit Utopia*, Songlines Gallery, Amsterdam, Netherlands, 20 April-7 June

• *Utopia Exhibition Adjunct to Documenta*, Kasel, Germany, July

• *Utopia Exhibition Adjunct to Documenta*, Fireworks Gallery, Brisbane, Queensland, Australia, July

• *Dreampower, Art of Contemporary Aboriginal Australia*, Museum Puri Lukisan, Ubud, Bali, Indonesia, 1-26 June

• *Dreampower, Art of Contemporary Aboriginal Australia*, Galeri Ardiyanto, Yogyakarta, Indonesia, 5-20 July

• *Dreampower, Art of Contemporary Aboriginal Australia*, The National Gallery of Indonesia, Jakarta, Indonesia, 4-16 August

• *Dreamings from the Home of the Mountain Devil Lizard*, Coo-ee Gallery, Sydney, New South Wales, Australia, 7 August-30 September

• *Mountain Devil Dreaming*, Japingka Gallery, Perth, Western Australia, Australia, 14 November-7 December
• *Recent Acquisitions*, National Gallery of Victoria, Melbourne, Victoria, Australia, November
• *14th NATSIAA Touring Exhibition*, Tandanya Aboriginal Cultural Institute, Adelaide, South Australia, Australia, 13 November-17 January 1998
• *John McCaughey Memorial Art Prize*, National Gallery of Victoria, Melbourne, Victoria, Australia, November-February 1998

1998 • *Our Country - Then & Now*, Gallerie Australis, South Australia, Australia, 7 March
• *Utopia Ladies*, Chapman Gallery, Canberra, Australian Capital Territory, Australia, 28 May
• *Expanse: Aboriginalities, spatialities and the politics of ecstasy*, Art Museum University of South Australia, Adelaide, South Australia, Australia, 4 September-3 October
• *Raiki Wara: Long Cloth from Aboriginal Australia and the Torres Strait*, National Gallery of Victoria, Melbourne, Victoria, Australia, 3 September-19 October
• *15th NATSIAA Touring Exhibition*, Museums and Art Galleries of the Northern Territory, Darwin, Northern Territory, Australia, 19 September-29 November
• *The Rodney Gooch Utopia Collection*, Riddock Regional Art Gallery, Mount Gambier, South Australia, Australia, 15-27 September
• *Belonging to Mother Earth - Indigenous Wisdom and Healing Conference*, Virginia Beach, Virginia, United States of America, 4-10 October
• *The Seppelts Contemporary Art Award Group Exhibition*, Museum of Contemporary Art, Sydney, New South Wales, Australia, 26 November-28 February 1999
• *Utopia Dreamings*, Japingka Gallery, Perth, Western Australia, Australia, 11 December-28 January 1999

1999 • *15th NATSIAA Touring Exhibition*, Gold Coast City Gallery, Surfers Paradise, Queensland, Australia, 18 June-25 July
• *15th NATSIAA Touring Exhibition*, Tandanya, Adelaide, South Australia, Australia, 14 August-3 October
• *15th NATSIAA Touring Exhibition*, RMIT Gallery, Melbourne, Victoria, Australia, 25 November-29 January
• *North by North East, Landscape & Ceremonial Paintings from Utopia*, Alcaston Gallery, Melbourne, Victoria, Australia, 8-30 July
• *SALA Week*, Gallerie Australis, Adelaide, South Australia, Australia, 1-8 August
• *Utopia: Ancient Cultures/New Forms*, Art Gallery of Western Australia, Perth, Western Australia, Australia, 16 October-9 January 2000
• *Utopian Visions: Emily Kngwarreye and the Women of Utopia*, Songlines Gallery, San Francisco, California, United States of America, 22 December-29 January 2000
• *Odyessy: A Journey into World Art*, Bicentennial Exhibition, Peabody-Essex Anthropology and Ethnology Museum, Harvard University, Salem, Massachusetts, United States of America, October-December

2000 • *Kurrunpa Marrka, Strong Spirit, New Directions in Contemporary Aboriginal Painting*, Songlines Gallery, San Francisco, California, United States of America, 10 February-1 April
• *From Appreciation to Appropriation: Indigenous Images and Influences in Australian Visual Art*, Flinders University, Adelaide, Australia, 5 March-26 April
• *The Return of Beauty*, Jam Factory, Adelaide, South Australia, Australia, 2 March-9 April
• *Beyond The Pale: Contemporary Indigenious Art, 2000 Adelaide Biennial of Australian Art*, Art Gallery of South Australia, Adelaide, South Australia, Australia, 3 March-16 April
• *Across: An Exhibition of Indigenous Art and Culture*, Institute of Arts, Australian National University, Canberra, Australian Capital Territory, Australia, 22 September-4 November
• *The Collection*, Gallerie Australis, Adelaide, South Australia, Australia, 4 March-30 April
• *Utopia*, Framed Gallery, Darwin, Northern Territory, Australia, 10-27 March
• *The Return of Beauty*, Object Galleries, Sydney, New South Wales, Australia, 29 April-12 June
• *SALA Week*, Gallerie Australis, Adelaide, South Australia, Australia, 5-13 August
• *Chemistry*, Art in South Australia 1990-2000, The Faulding Exhibition, Art Gallery of South Australia, Adelaide, South Australia, Australia, 16 September-5 November
• *Two Women Dreaming: The Emergence of International Style Indigenous Painting (Kathleen Petyarre & Gloria Petyarre)*, Songlines Gallery, San Francisco, California, United States of America, 4 November-6 January 2001
• *Across: An Exhibition of Indigenous Art and Culture*, Australian National University, Canberra School of Art Gallery, Canberra, Australian Capital Territory, Australia, 22 September-4 November
• *All About Art*, Alcaston Gallery, Melbourne, Victoria, Australia, 12 September-13 October

2001 • *Spirituality & Australian Aboriginal Art*, Touring Exhibition, various venues, Madrid and throughout Spain, 1 March-31 December
• *Art on Steel*, BHP Art, National Tour of Australia
• *Across: An Exhibition of Indigenous Art and Culture*, Counihan Gallery of Art, Melbourne, Victoria, Australia, 10 May-3 June
• *Across: An exhibition of Indigenous Art and Culture*, Flinders University City Gallery, Adelaide, South Australia, Australia, 23 June-28 July
• *Across: An Exhibition of Indigenous Art and Culture*, Lawrence Wilson Gallery, Perth, Western Australia, Australia, 14 August-28 October
• *DREAMTIME: Zeitgenossische Aboriginal Art*, 'The Dark and The Light', Sammlung Essl, Klosterneuberg, Vienna, Austria, May
• *A Few of My Favourite Things: DREAMTIME Complimentary Exhibition*, Fire-Works Gallery, Brisbane, Queensland, Australia, June

Awards

1996 • Joint second prize, Open Award Category, The Third National Aboriginal & Torres Strait Islander Heritage Commission Art Award, Canberra, Australian Capital Territory, Australia
• Overall winner of the Telstra 13th National Aboriginal & Torres Strait Islander Art Award, Darwin, Northern Territory, Australia

1997 • Overall winner of the Visy Board Art Prize, the Barossa Vintage Festival Art Show, Nurioopta, South Australia, Australia

1998 • Finalist, 1998 Seppelts Contemporary Art Award - Visual Art, Museum of Contemporary Art, Sydney, New South Wales, Australia
• Winner, People's Choice Award, 1998 Seppelts Contemporary Art Award, Museum of Contemporary Art, Sydney, New South Wales, Australia

Selected Collections

PAINTINGS

Collection of HM Queen Elizabeth II
National Gallery of Australia, Canberra, Australian Capital Territory, Australia
The Kerry Stokes Collection, Perth, Western Australia, Australia
The Museum & Art Galleries of the Northern Territory, Darwin, Northern Territory, Australia
Art Gallery of South Australia, Adelaide, South Australia, Australia
Flinders University Art Museum, Adelaide, South Australia, Australia
The Kluge-Ruhe Collection, University of West Virginia, Virginia, United States of America
The Kelton Foundation, Los Angeles, California, United States of America
The Levi-Kaplan Collection, Seattle, Washington, United States of America
ATSIC Collection, Adelaide, South Australia, Australia
National Gallery of Victoria, Melbourne, Victoria, Australia
Museum Puri Lukisan, Ubud, Bali, Indonesia
University of South Australia Art Museum, Adelaide, South Australia, Australia
Riddoch Regional Art Gallery, Mount Gambier, South Australia, Australia
Edith Cowan University, Perth, Western Australia, Australia
Collection de Musée des Arts d'Afrique et d'Oceanie, Paris, France
Peabody-Essex Anthropology and Ethnology Museum, Harvard University, Salem, Massachusetts, United States of America
James and Jaqui Erskine Collection, Sydney, New South Wales, Australia
The Essl Collection, Sammlung Essl, Vienna, Austria

PRINTS AND WOOD-BLOCKS

The National Gallery of Australia, Canberra, Australian Capital Territory, Australia
Museum & Art Galleries of the Northern Territory, Darwin, Northern Territory, Australia

BATIK

The Holmes à Court Collection, Western Australia, Australia
The Riddoch Gallery, Mount Gambier, South Australia, Australia

Artist-in-residence

1997 • Art Gallery of South Australia, Desert Artists-in-Residence, Adelaide, South Australia, Australia, January
• Museum Puri Lukisan, Ubud, Bali, Indonesia, June

Commissions

1997 • The John McCaughey Memorial Art Prize, National Gallery of Victoria, Melbourne, Victoria, Australia

Expositions

1982 • Sydney Craft Expo, Sydney, New South Wales, Australia

1996 • Australian Contemporary Art Fair 5, Melbourne, paintings by Kathleen Petyarre, 1-4 October, presented by Alcaston Gallery, Melbourne, Victoria, Australia

1998 • Australian Contemporary Art Fair 6, Melbourne, paintings by Kathleen Petyarre, 4-8 October, presented by Alcaston Gallery, Melbourne, Victoria, Australia

1999 • Art 1999 Chicago, Navy Pier, Chicago, Illinois, United States of America, 7-10 May, paintings by Kathleen Petyarre & Emily Kame Kngwarreye. Presented by Songlines Gallery of Amsterdam, Netherlands and San Francisco, California, United States of America
• SF2, San Francisco International Art Exposition 2, paintings by Kathleen Petyarre and Emily Kngwarreye, Fort Mason Centre, San Francisco, United States of America, 30 September-4 October. Presented by Songlines Gallery of Amsterdam, Netherlands and San Francisco, California, United States of America
• Art Chicago 2000, Navy Pier, Chicago, Illinois, United States of America, 12-15 May. Presented by Songlines Gallery of Amsterdam, Netherlands and San Francisco, California, United States of America
• SF3, San Francisco International Art Exposition 3, Fort Mason Centre, San Francisco, United States of America, 22 September-25 September. Presented by Songlines Gallery of Amsterdam, Netherlands and San Francisco, California, United States of America

2000 • Australian Contemporary Art Fair 7, Melbourne, paintings by Kathleen Petyarrre, presented by Alcaston Gallery, Exhibition Hall, Melbourne, Victoria, Australia, 4-8 October

Scholarships

1998 • Australian Delegate, Belonging to Mother Earth - Indigenous Wisdom and Healing Conference, Virginia Beach, Virginia, United States of America, 4-10 October

REFERENCES AND FURTHER READING

Baddeley, Clare (ed.), *1999, Motif & Meaning: Aboriginal Influences in Australian Art 1930–1970*, Ballarat Fine Art Gallery: Ballarat, Australia

Bentley, P.J. and F.C. Blumer, 1962, 'Uptake of water by the lizard, *Moloch horridus*', *Nature* 194 pp. 699-700, Macmillian Journals: London, United Kingdom

Best, Susan, 2000, 'You are now on Aboriginal land', (ed.) Harper, Jenny, *Pre/dictions: the Role of Art at the End of the Millennium: Proceedings of the Art Association of Australia and New Zealand held in Wellington, 2–5 December 1999*, Victoria University: Wellington, New Zealand, pp. 18–25

Boulter, Michael, 1991, *The Art of Utopia: A New Direction in Contemporary Aboriginal Art*, Craftsman House: Sydney, Australia

Brody, Anne Marie, 1989, *Utopia Women's Paintings: The First Works on Canvas, A Summer Project*, Catalogue No.7, Heytesbury Holdings Ltd: Perth, Australia

Brody, Anne Marie, 1990, *Utopia - A Picture Story, 88 Silk Batiks from the Robert Holmes à Court Collection*, Heytesbury Holdings Ltd: Perth, Australia

Brody, Anne Marie, 1990, *Contemporary Aboriginal Art from the Robert Holmes à Court Collection*, Heytesbury Holdings Ltd: Perth, Australia

Butler, Sally, 'The role of the aura at the end of the millennium', (ed.) Harper, Jenny, *Pre/dictions: the Role of Art at the End of the Millennium: Proceedings of the Art Asociation of Australia and New Zealand held in Wellington, 2–5 December 1999*, Victoria University: Wellington, New Zealand, pp. 44–48

Butler, Rex, April-June 2001, 'All and Nothing, Kathleen Petyarre's Sublime "X"', *Australian Art Collector*, 16, Gadfly Media: Sydney, Australia, pp. 90-93

Campfire Group (eds), 2001, *Dreamtime: The Dark and the Light*, Sammlung Essl: Vienna, Austria

Cataldi, Lee, 1998, They don't need to read, they can paint: a critique of the thesis of Jennifer Biddle's paper 'When not writing is writing', unpublished lecture, Flinders University, Adelaide, Australia.

Cossey, David, 1997, *Dreampower, Art of Contemporary Aboriginal Australia*, Museum Art International: Adelaide, Australia

Devitt, Jeannie, June 1988, Contemporary Aboriginal Women and Subsistence in Remote, Arid Australia, unpublished PhD thesis, Department of Anthropology and Sociology, University of Queensland, St Lucia, Australia

Eades, Diana, 1991, 'Communicative Strategies in Aboriginal English', (ed.) Romaine, Suzanne, *Language in Australia*, Cambridge University Press: Cambridge, UK, and Melbourne, Australia

Green, Jenny, 1998, 'Singing the Silk: Utopia Batik', (ed.) Ryan, Judith, *Raiki Wara: Long cloth from Aboriginal Australia and the Torres Strait*, National Gallery of Victoria: Melbourne, Australia, pp. 38–49

Greer, Germaine, 1997, 'Raiders of the lost art', Melbourne *Age* Extra/Features, 6 December, p. 6

James, Bruce, 1999 'Spot the Difference', *Sydney Morning Herald*: Spectrum, 13 November, p. 14s

Johnson, Vivien, 1997, *Michael Jagamara Nelson*, Craftsman House: Sydney, Australia

Landsam, David, March 1996, 'Aboriginal Art: Australia's hidden resource', *Art Monthly Australia*, No. 87, Art Monthly Australia Pty Ltd: Canberra, Australia pp. 4–5

McCulloch, Susan, 1997, 'Revealed: black art scandal', *Weekend Australian*, 15–16 November, p. 1

McCulloch, Susan, 1997, 'Lauded black artist confesses, it's not my work', *Australian*, 23 December, p. 1

McDonald, Colin, 1998, 'Chairman's Message', West, Margie (ed.), *Telstra 15th National Aboriginal & Torres Strait Islander Art Award Catalogue, 1998*, Museum and Art Gallery of the Northern Territory: Darwin, Australia, pp. 4-6

McEvilley, Thomas, with G. Roger Denson, 1996, *Capacity: History, the World, and the Self in Contemporary Art Criticism*, G+B Arts International: Amsterdam, The Netherlands.

Mellor, Doreen, 1998, 'Kathleen Petyarre', *Seppelt Contemporary Art Awards, MCA 1998 Catalogue*, Museum of Contemporary Art: Sydney, Australia, pp. 14-18

Mendelssohn, Joanna, 1997, 'The great artistic "crime" of collaboration', *Australian* Opinion, 24 December, p. 11

Michaels, Eric, 1988, 'Bad Aboriginal Art', *Art & Text* 28, March–May, pp. 59–73

Murray, Julia, 1998, 'Utopia Batik: The halcyon days 1978–82', (ed.) Ryan, Judith, *Raiki Wara: Long cloth from Aboriginal Australia and the Torres Strait*, National Gallery of Victoria: Melbourne, Australia, pp. 50–55

Nicholls, Christine, 1998, Nicknaming and Graffiti-Writing Practices at Lajamanu N.T.: A Post-Ethnographic Sociological Fiction, unpublished Ph.D. thesis, Macquarie University, Sydney, Australia

Nicholls, Christine, 1998, 'A Dreaming nightmare over', Adelaide *Advertiser* Comment, 25 April, p. 49

Nicholls, Christine, 1998, 'The devil Kathleen knows', Adelaide *Advertiser*, 1 August, p. 49

Nicholls, Christine, October 1998, 'Kathleen Petyarre and the heroic odyssey of Arnkerrth', *Art Monthly Australia* No. 114, Art Monthly Australia Ltd: Canberra, Australia, pp. 7–10

Nicholls, Christine, August–November 1998, 'Kathleen Petyarre's *Annus Horribilis* comes to an end', *State of the Arts: South Australia*, and other Australian issues, State of the Art Publications: Kings Cross, Sydney, Australia

Nicholls, Christine, 1999, 'Kathleen Petyarre: An artist for our times', *Paintings by Kathleen Petyarre*, Gallerie Australis catalogue: Adelaide,

Australia. (Also reproduced in *The Return of Beauty* catalogue, The Jam Factory, for the Adelaide Festival of Arts 2000, pp. 22–24.)

Nicholls, Christine, November 1999, 'Kathleen Petyarre: Artist', *Australian Way*, Qantas Inflight Magazine, The Showcase, Australians in the Spotlight, BRW Media: Melbourne, Australia, p. 118

Nicholls, Christine, December 1999, 'An introduction to the women painters of Utopia, Northern Territory', *Journal of the Anthropological Society of South Australia*, vol. 32: Adelaide, Australia, pp. 1–27

Nicholls, Christine, 2000, 'Kathleen Petyarre', (ed.) Croft, Brenda L. *Beyond The Pale: Contemporary Indigenous Art, 2000 Adelaide Biennial of Australian Art*, Art Gallery Board of South Australia: Adelaide, Australia, pp. 65–70

Nicholls, Christine, 2000, *From Appreciation to Appropriation: Indigenous Influences and Images in Australian Visual Arts*, exhibition (5 March–16 April) catalogue, Flinders University Art Museum: Adelaide, Australia

Nicholls, Christine, 2000, 'Kathleen Petyarre', (eds) Kleinert, Sylvia, and Neale, Margo, *The Oxford Companion to Aboriginal Art and Culture*, Oxford University Press: UK and Australia, p. 672

Nicholls, Christine, 2001, 'Espiritualidad Y Arte Aborigen Australiano', ('Spirituality and Australian Aboriginal Art'), catalogue essay for exhibition of the same name, Comunidad di Madrid, Cosejeria de Cultura, Direccion General Promocion Cultural: Madrid, Spain

Nicholls, Christine, April 2001, 'Home and Away with Kathleen and Violet Petyarre, or, Travels with my aunts', *Art Monthly Australia*, No. 138, Art Monthly Australia Ltd: Canberra, Australia, pp. 16–20

Nicholls, Christine, May 2001, 'Genius of Place: The Work of Kathleen Petyarre, 9 May-22 July 2001', room brochure to accompany exhibition of the same name, Museum of Contemporary Art: Sydney, Australia

North, Ian, 1998, *Expanse: Aboriginalities, Spatialities and the Politics of Ecstasy*, University of South Australia Art Museum: Adelaide, Australia

North, Ian, forthcoming 2001, 'StarAboriginality', Charles Green (ed.), *Postcolonial + Art: Where Now?*, Artspace Visual Arts Centre: Sydney, Australia

Pianka, E.R, 1997, 'Australia's thorny devil', *Reptiles* 5 (11), Fancy Publications Inc., Mission Viego, California USA: pp. 14–23

Pianka, E.R. and W.L. Hodges, 1998, 'Horned lizards', *Reptiles* 6 (6) Fancy Publications Inc., Mission Viego, California USA: pp. 48–63

Pianka, E.R. and W.S. Parker, 1975, 'Ecology of horned lizards: A review with special reference to *Phrynosoma platyrhinos*', *Copeia*, American Society of Ichthyologists and Herpetologists (ASIH), Lawrence, Kansas USA: pp. 141–162

Pianka, E.R. and H.D. Pianka, 1970, 'The ecology of *Moloch horridus* (Lacertilia: Agamidae) in Western Australia', *Copeia*, American Society of Ichthyologists and Herpetologists (ASIH), Lawrence, Kansas USA: pp. 90–103

Pianka, G.A., E.R. Pianka, and G.G. Thompson, 1996, 'Egg laying by thorny devils (*Moloch horridus*) under natural conditions in the Great Victoria desert', *Journal of the Royal Society of Western Australia*, 79, Perth, Australia: pp. 195–197

Pianka, G.A., E.R. Pianka, and G.G. Thompson, 1998, 'Natural history of thorny devils *Moloch horridus* (Lacertilia: Agamidae) in the Great Victoria desert', *Journal of the Royal Society of Western Australia*, 81 Perth, Australia: pp. 183–190

Richardson, Nick, forthcoming 2001, An Historical Survey of State Schooling in the Sandover River Region of Central Australia During the Twentieth Century, MA thesis, Flinders University, Adelaide, Australia

Ryan, Judith, 1998, *Raiki Wara, Long Cloth from Aboriginal Australia and the Torres Strait*, National Gallery of Victoria: Melbourne, Australia

Toohey, Justice John, 1980, *Aboriginal Land Rights (Northern Territory) Act 1976*, Anmatjirra and Alyawarra Land Claim to Utopia Pastoral Lease, Report by the Aboriginal Land Commissioner to the Minister for Aboriginal Affairs and to the Administrator of the Northern Territory, Australian Government Printer: Australian Capital Territory, Australia

West, Margie (ed.), 2000, 'Transitions: 17 Years of the National Aboriginal and Torres Strait Islander Art Award', *Museum and Art Gallery of Northern Territory Travelling Exhibition Catalogue*, Darwin, Australia, pp. 38-45

Wright, Felicity and Frances Morphy (eds.), 1999, *The Art & Craft Centre Story* (2 vols.), Aboriginal and Torres Strait Islander Commission: Canberra, Australia